PETRA TRAVEL GUIDE 2024

Bill Bryson

Copyright © 2024 by Bill Bryson. All rights reserved. No part of this book may be reproduced or transmitted in any form or by any means, electronic or mechanical, including photocopying, recording, or by any information storage and retrieval system, without written permission from the author, except for the inclusion of brief quotations in a review

TABLE OF CONTENTS

1.0 Introduction
1.1 Overview of Petra
1.2 Brief History and Culture
1.3 Why Visit Petra

2.0 Planning Your Trip
2.1 Best Time to Visit
2.2 Visa and Entry Requirements
2.3 Currency and Banking
2.4 Health and safety tips
2.5 Packing Essentials

3.0 Transportation
3.1 Getting to Petra
3.2 Getting Around Petra
3.3 Public Transportation

4.0 Accommodation
4.1 Luxury hotel
4.2 Budget-Friendly Options

4.3 Airbnb and Vacation Rentals
4.4 Hostels

5.0 Shopping Guide
5.1 Shopping mall
5.2 Local Markets
5.3 Unique Souvenirs

6.0 Cuisine and Dining
6.1 Local Petra Dishes
6.2 Popular Restaurants and Cafes
6.3 Street Food Experiences

7.0 Exploring Petra
7.1 Overview Map of Petra
7.2 Main Attractions
7.3 Lesser-Known Sites
7.4 Guided Tours vs. Solo Exploration
7.5 Activities in Petra

8.0 Hiking Trails
8.1 Horseback Riding

8.2 Camel Rides
8.3 Sunset and Night Tours

9.0 Cultural and Historical Insights
9.1 Nabatean Civilization
9.2 Architectural Marvels
9.3 Religious Significance
9.4 Petra in Popular Culture

10.0 Practical Tips
10.1 Language and Communication
10.2 Photography Etiquette
10.3 General emergency contact in Petra

11.0 Sample Itineraries
11.1 One Week Itinerary
11.2 Weekend Getaway
11.3 Budget Traveler's Guide

12.0 Conclusion

WELCOME NOTE

Hello dear friend, Whether you're a history buff, an intrepid explorer, or simply someone with a thirst for adventure, we're thrilled to have you join us on this journey to one of the most awe-inspiring destinations on the planet – Petra!

As you embark on your Petra adventure, get ready to step back in time and immerse yourself in the rich beauty of history, culture, and natural beauty that this ancient wonder has to offer. From the moment you enter the narrow Siq, with its towering sandstone walls whispering tales of civilizations past, to the breathtaking reveal of the iconic Treasury, every step you take in Petra is a moment to treasure.

But hey, we're not just here for the history lesson – although Petra's got plenty of that! We're also here to soak up the vibes, mingle with locals, and uncover those hidden gems that make travel oh-so-exciting. So whether you're snapping selfies at the Monastery, bargaining for souvenirs in the local markets, or savoring a delicious falafel wrap from a street vendor, remember to soak it all in and embrace the magic of the moment.

And hey, if you ever need a helping hand, some insider tips, or just a friendly face to chat with, we've got your back! Our Petra travel guide is packed with all the info you need to make the most of your adventure, from must-see attractions to off-the-beaten-path gems and everything in between.

So, fellow adventurers, get ready to write your own chapter in the story of Petra – a tale of wonder, discovery, and unforgettable experiences. We're so excited to have you along for the ride, and we can't wait to see where this journey takes us!

Safe travels and happy exploring!

1.0 Introduction

1.1 Overview of Petra

Petra, often referred to as the "Rose City," is an ancient archaeological site located in southern Jordan, encompassing a vast and awe-inspiring landscape of rock-cut architecture, tombs, temples, and intricate carvings. Nestled within the rugged mountains of Wadi Musa, Petra served as the capital of the Nabatean Kingdom from around the 4th century BCE to the 2nd century CE, flourishing as a vital trade hub and center of commerce along ancient caravan routes.

1.1.1 Historical Significance

The history of Petra dates back over two millennia, with evidence of human habitation in the region dating back to prehistoric times. However, it was the Nabateans, an industrious Arab people, who transformed Petra into a thriving city during their heyday. The Nabateans were skilled traders who capitalized on Petra's strategic location along the Silk Road, establishing it as a crucial nexus for trade between the Mediterranean world, Arabia, and the Far East.

1.1.2 Architectural Marvels

One of the most remarkable features of Petra is its unique architectural heritage, characterized by its stunning rock-cut facades and structures carved directly into the rose-red sandstone cliffs. The most iconic of these structures is undoubtedly the Treasury (Al-Khazneh), with its intricate façade adorned with intricate carvings and columns. Other notable landmarks include the Street of Facades, the Royal Tombs, and the Monastery (Ad Deir), each offering a glimpse into the ingenuity and craftsmanship of the Nabatean civilization.

1.1.3 Geological Formation

Petra's geological formation is as remarkable as its human history. The city is situated within a narrow gorge known as the Siq, which stretches for over a kilometer and features towering cliffs that soar up to 200 meters in height. This natural canyon served as the main entrance to Petra and provided the Nabateans with a natural defense against invaders. The geological formations surrounding Petra, including the towering sandstone cliffs and rocky outcrops, contribute to its dramatic and otherworldly beauty.

1.1.4 Cultural Significance

Beyond its architectural splendor, Petra holds immense cultural and historical significance. The site's diverse cultural influences reflect the interplay between various civilizations that inhabited the region over the centuries, including the Nabateans, Romans, Byzantines, and Arabs. Additionally, Petra's inclusion as a UNESCO World Heritage Site in 1985 further underscores its importance as a global treasure and a testament to human ingenuity and creativity.

1.1.5 Modern Exploration and Tourism

In modern times, Petra has become one of Jordan's most visited tourist destinations, attracting travelers from around the world eager to experience its ancient wonders firsthand. While Petra's popularity has grown steadily over the years, efforts have been made to balance conservation with sustainable tourism practices to ensure the preservation of this cultural heritage site for future generations.

Petra stands as a testament to the ingenuity, resilience, and creativity of the ancient Nabateans, whose legacy continues to captivate and inspire visitors to this day. With its awe-inspiring architecture, rich history, and breathtaking natural beauty, Petra remains a timeless marvel and a must-visit destination for travelers seeking to immerse themselves in the wonders of the ancient world.

1.2 Brief History and Culture

Petra's history is as rich and fascinating as its breathtaking architecture and natural surroundings. From its ancient origins as a Nabatean capital to its subsequent occupation by various civilizations, Petra's cultural heritage is a beauty woven with the threads of time, conquest, and trade.

1.2.1 Nabatean Civilization

The story of Petra begins with the Nabateans, a nomadic Arab tribe who settled in the region around the 6th century BCE. Originally pastoralists, the Nabateans were drawn to the area's strategic location along trade routes linking Arabia, Egypt, and the Levant. Over time, they transformed Petra into a bustling city and capital of their kingdom, establishing a sophisticated network of cisterns, dams, and water channels to harness the region's scarce water resources.

The Nabateans were renowned for their skill in trade, cultivating prosperous commercial ties with neighboring empires such as the Roman Republic and the Hellenistic kingdoms. Their strategic location along the Incense Route, which connected southern Arabia to the Mediterranean world, allowed them to amass wealth and exert significant influence in the ancient Near East.

1.2.2 Roman and Byzantine Rule

In 106 CE, Petra fell under Roman rule following the annexation of the Nabatean Kingdom by Emperor Trajan. Under Roman administration, Petra continued to thrive as a regional center of commerce and culture, with the construction of monumental buildings, temples, and theaters reflecting Roman architectural influence.

During the Byzantine period, Petra experienced a resurgence as a Christian pilgrimage site, with churches and monasteries dotting the landscape. However, with the decline of the Roman Empire and the shift in trade routes away from Petra, the city gradually declined in importance, eventually fading into obscurity by the early Islamic period.

1.2.3 Rediscovery and Archaeological Exploration

Petra's existence was known to local Bedouin tribes and European travelers throughout the Middle Ages, but it wasn't until the early 19th century that the city captured the imagination of the Western world. In 1812, Swiss explorer Johann Ludwig Burckhardt disguised himself as a Muslim pilgrim and successfully infiltrated

Petra, bringing it to the attention of European scholars and adventurers.

Subsequent archaeological expeditions uncovered the extent of Petra's ancient splendor, revealing an array of temples, tombs, and monuments carved into the sandstone cliffs. Excavations conducted throughout the 20th and 21st centuries have shed further light on Petra's history and culture, uncovering evidence of its multicultural past and the daily lives of its inhabitants.

1.2.4 Cultural Legacy and UNESCO World Heritage Site

In recognition of its significance as a cultural treasure, Petra was designated a UNESCO World Heritage Site in 1985, ensuring its preservation for future generations. Today, Petra stands as a symbol of human ingenuity and creativity, a testament to the enduring legacy of the Nabateans and the diverse civilizations that once called this ancient city home.

Visitors to Petra are captivated not only by its stunning architecture and natural beauty but also by the tangible sense of history that permeates every corner of the site. From the towering cliffs of the Siq to the majestic facades of the Treasury and the Monastery, Petra continues to inspire wonder and awe, inviting travelers to embark on a journey through the annals of time.

1.3 Why Visit Petra

Petra is more than just an archaeological site; it's an experience that transcends time and transports visitors to a bygone era of majesty, innovation, and cultural exchange. Here are several compelling reasons why Petra should be on every traveler's bucket list:

1.3.1. Architectural Marvels: Petra's most iconic feature is undoubtedly its breathtaking architecture, characterized by intricately carved facades, tombs, and temples hewn directly into the rose-red sandstone cliffs. From the imposing Treasury (Al-Khazneh) to the towering Monastery (Ad Deir), Petra's structures showcase the ingenuity and craftsmanship of the ancient Nabateans, leaving visitors in awe of their architectural prowess.

1.3.2. Rich History: Petra's history spans millennia, from its origins as a Nabatean capital to its subsequent occupation by the Romans, Byzantines, and other civilizations. Exploring Petra allows visitors to delve into the ancient past and gain insight into the vibrant cultural beauty of the region, from its role as a vital trade hub to its significance as a center of religious pilgrimage.

1.3.3. Natural Beauty:

Nestled within a rugged canyon known as the Siq, Petra's setting is as stunning as its architecture. The towering sandstone cliffs, winding paths, and hidden gorges create a sense of adventure and discovery, beckoning visitors to explore its hidden treasures. Whether admiring the play of light and shadow in the Siq or marveling at the panoramic views from the High Place of Sacrifice, Petra's natural beauty is unparalleled.

1.3.4. Cultural Significance:

As a UNESCO World Heritage Site, Petra holds immense cultural significance as a testament to human creativity and resilience. Its inclusion on the prestigious list ensures its preservation for future generations and underscores its importance as a global heritage site. By visiting Petra, travelers contribute to the ongoing efforts to safeguard this ancient marvel and promote cross-cultural understanding.

1.3.5. Spiritual Exploration: For centuries, Petra has been revered as a sacred site by various civilizations, including the Nabateans and later Christian pilgrims. Today, visitors can still sense the spiritual aura that pervades the city, whether marveling at the intricate rock-cut tombs or contemplating the ancient rituals performed at the site. Petra offers a unique opportunity for spiritual reflection and introspection amid its awe-inspiring surroundings.

1.3.6. Adventure and Exploration: Petra is a paradise for adventurers and history enthusiasts alike, with countless opportunities for hiking, camel rides, and guided tours. Whether traversing the rugged terrain of the Petra Archaeological Park or embarking on a journey to nearby sites such as Wadi Rum and Little Petra, visitors can immerse themselves in the thrill of discovery and exploration.

1.3.7. Cultural Exchange: Petra's history is a testament to the diverse cultural exchanges that have shaped the region over the centuries. By visiting Petra, travelers have the opportunity to engage with local communities, learn about Jordanian culture and traditions, and forge connections with people from around the world. Whether chatting with Bedouin guides or sampling traditional Jordanian cuisine, Petra offers a rich beauty of cultural experiences.

Petra is not just a destination; it's an unparalleled journey through time and culture, offering visitors a chance to connect with the past, explore hidden wonders, and create lasting memories. Whether you're drawn to its architectural splendor, natural beauty, or rich history, Petra promises an unforgettable experience that will leave a lasting impression on your heart and mind.

2.0 Planning Your Trip

2.1 Best Time to Visit

Choosing the ideal time to visit Petra is crucial for maximizing your experience and enjoyment of this ancient wonder. Several factors, including weather, crowd levels, and special events, should be considered when planning your trip to Petra.

2.1.1. Weather Considerations:

Spring (March to May): Spring is widely regarded as the best time to visit Petra. During this season, the weather is mild and pleasant, with temperatures ranging from 15°C to 25°C (59°F to 77°F) on average. The landscape comes alive with vibrant wildflowers, and the surrounding hillsides are carpeted with greenery, making it an ideal time for outdoor exploration and photography.

Autumn (September to November): Similar to spring, autumn offers favorable weather conditions for visiting Petra. Temperatures are comfortable, ranging from 15°C to 30°C (59°F to 86°F), and the crowds tend to be smaller compared to the peak summer months. Autumn is an excellent time to enjoy hiking and sightseeing without the scorching heat of summer.

2.1.2. Crowd Levels:

Off-Peak Season (December to February): Winter is considered the off-peak season for tourism in Petra, with fewer visitors and lower accommodation prices. While temperatures can be chilly, ranging from 5°C to 15°C (41°F to 59°F), this is an excellent time to explore Petra without the crowds and enjoy a more intimate experience with the site's wonders.

Peak Season (June to August): Summer is the peak tourist season in Petra, attracting large crowds of visitors from around the world. However, the scorching heat can be challenging to endure, with temperatures soaring above 35°C (95°F) during the day. It's essential to stay hydrated and seek shade when exploring Petra in the summer months.

2.1.3. Special Events:

Petra by Night: One of the highlights of visiting Petra is experiencing Petra by Night, a magical event where the ancient city is illuminated by thousands of candles. This enchanting experience takes place several times a week and offers a unique opportunity to see Petra's iconic monuments in a different light. It's advisable to check the schedule and plan your visit accordingly.

Cultural Festivals: Throughout the year, Petra hosts various cultural festivals and events that celebrate Jordanian heritage, music, and arts. These festivals provide a chance to immerse yourself in local culture and traditions while exploring the ancient wonders of Petra. Be sure to inquire about upcoming events when planning your visit.

Ultimately, the best time to visit Petra depends on your preferences, interests, and tolerance for weather conditions. Spring and autumn are generally considered the optimal seasons for exploring Petra, offering pleasant weather and fewer crowds. However, visiting during the off-peak winter months can also provide a unique and rewarding experience, while summer may be best avoided due to extreme heat and high tourist numbers. Regardless of when you choose to visit, Petra promises an unforgettable journey through history, culture, and natural beauty.

2.2 Visa and Entry Requirements

Before embarking on your journey to Petra, it's essential to familiarize yourself with the visa and entry requirements for visiting Jordan. Here's an extensive guide to help you navigate the process:

2.2.1. Visa Types:

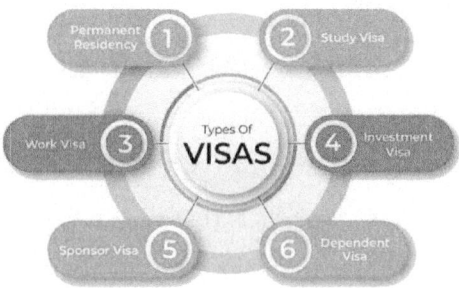

Tourist Visa: Most visitors to Jordan will require a tourist visa to enter the country. The tourist visa allows for stays of up to 30 days and can be obtained upon arrival at Jordanian airports and land border crossings.

Single-Entry Visa: This type of visa allows for a single entry into Jordan and is valid for one month from the date of entry.

Multiple-Entry Visa: Travelers planning to leave and re-enter Jordan multiple times within a specified period may opt for a multiple-entry visa. This type of visa is typically valid for three months from the date of entry.

Transit Visa: Travelers transiting through Jordan en route to another destination may be eligible for a transit visa, allowing for a short stay in the country.

2.2.2. Visa Requirements:

Passport: All travelers to Jordan must possess a passport valid for at least six months beyond the intended date of departure from the country.

Visa Application Form: Upon arrival at a Jordanian port of entry, travelers will be required to complete a visa application form, which is usually provided by immigration authorities.

Visa Fees: Visa fees vary depending on the type and duration of the visa. Payment is typically made in cash in Jordanian dinars (JOD) or other accepted currencies.

Proof of Sufficient Funds: Immigration authorities may require travelers to provide proof of sufficient funds to cover their stay in Jordan, such as bank statements or a valid credit card.

Return Ticket: Travelers may be asked to provide proof of a return or onward ticket from Jordan as a condition of entry.

2.2.3. Visa Extensions:

Travelers wishing to extend their stay in Jordan beyond the initial visa validity period may apply for a visa extension at the nearest immigration office. Visa extensions are subject to approval by Jordanian authorities and may incur additional fees.

2.2.4. Visa-Free Entry:

Citizens of certain countries are eligible for visa-free entry to Jordan for specified periods. These countries include members of the Gulf Cooperation Council (GCC), European Union (EU), and several others. It's advisable to check the latest visa requirements and exemptions before traveling to Jordan.

2.2.5. Entry Requirements for Petra:

Once you have obtained the necessary visa to enter Jordan, there are no additional entry requirements specifically for visiting Petra. However, visitors should be prepared to present their passports and valid visas at Petra's entrance gates for verification by park authorities.

Navigating the visa and entry requirements for visiting Petra and Jordan is a straightforward process, but it's essential to plan ahead and ensure that you have the necessary documentation before your trip. By familiarizing yourself with the visa types, requirements, and regulations, you can enjoy a smooth and hassle-free journey to Petra, where you'll be greeted with ancient wonders, breathtaking landscapes, and warm Jordanian hospitality.

2.3 Currency and Banking

Understanding the currency and banking system in Jordan is essential for travelers planning to visit Petra and explore the country's other attractions. Here's an extensive guide to help you navigate currency exchange, banking services, and financial matters during your stay in Jordan:

2.3.1. Currency:

Jordanian Dinar (JOD): The official currency of Jordan is the Jordanian Dinar, abbreviated as JOD or JD. The dinar is divided into 1000 fils. Banknotes are available in denominations of 1, 5, 10, 20, and 50 dinars, while coins are available in denominations of 1, 5, 10, 25, and 50 fils, as well as 1 dinar.

Foreign Currency: While the Jordanian Dinar is the primary currency used in Jordan, major foreign currencies such as US dollars and euros are widely accepted in hotels, restaurants, and tourist establishments, especially in popular tourist destinations like Petra and Amman. However, it's advisable to carry some Jordanian Dinar for smaller purchases and transactions.

Currency Exchange:

Currency exchange services are available at banks, exchange bureaus, and hotels throughout Jordan. Banks typically offer competitive exchange rates, although they may charge higher fees and commissions compared to exchange bureaus. It's advisable to compare rates and fees before exchanging currency to ensure the best deal.

ATMs: ATMs are widely available in major cities and tourist areas in Jordan, including Petra and Amman. Most ATMs accept international credit and debit cards, including Visa, MasterCard, and Maestro. Withdrawals are typically processed in Jordanian Dinar, and some ATMs may offer the option to withdraw cash in foreign currency.

Credit Cards:

Credit cards, particularly Visa and MasterCard, are widely accepted in hotels, restaurants, shops, and other establishments in Jordan, especially in urban areas like Amman. However, in more remote areas and smaller towns, cash may be the preferred method of payment. It's always a good idea to carry some cash for emergencies and smaller purchases.

Traveler's Checks: While traveler's checks were once a popular form of currency for international travel, their use has declined significantly in recent years. Many businesses in Jordan no longer accept traveler's checks, and exchange services may be limited. It's advisable to carry cash or use credit/debit cards instead.

2.3.2 Banking Services:

Banks: Jordan is home to several local and international banks, including Arab Bank, Jordan Commercial Bank, and Housing Bank for Trade and Finance. Banks in Jordan offer a wide range of financial services, including currency exchange, ATM access, wire transfers, and foreign currency accounts.

Banking Hours: Banking hours in Jordan typically run from Sunday to Thursday, with branches open from 8:30 AM to 3:00 PM. Some branches may also offer extended hours in the evenings or on Fridays and Saturdays in major cities like Amman.

Online Banking: Many banks in Jordan offer online banking services, allowing customers to manage their accounts, transfer funds, pay bills, and access other banking services remotely. Online banking platforms are usually available in English and Arabic for the convenience of international customers.

Navigating the currency and banking system in Jordan is relatively straightforward, with a range of options available for exchanging currency, accessing cash, and managing finances during your stay. By familiarizing yourself with the local currency, banking services, and payment methods, you can enjoy a seamless and hassle-free travel experience in Jordan, whether you're exploring Petra's ancient wonders or soaking up the vibrant culture of Amman.

2.4 Health and safety tips

Traveling to Petra, like any destination, requires careful consideration of health and safety precautions to ensure a smooth and enjoyable experience. Here are some extensive health and safety tips to keep in mind while visiting Petra:

2.4.1. Pre-Travel Health Preparation:

Consult a healthcare professional: Before traveling to Petra, it's advisable to schedule a visit with your doctor or a travel medicine specialist to discuss any necessary vaccinations, medications, or health precautions based on your individual health status and travel itinerary.

Obtain travel insurance: Consider purchasing comprehensive travel insurance that includes coverage for medical emergencies, trip cancellations, and other unforeseen events. Verify that your policy covers activities such as hiking and adventure sports, especially if you plan to engage in these activities in Petra.

2.4.2. General Safety Tips:

Research travel advisories: Stay informed about current travel advisories and safety recommendations for Jordan issued by your country's government or reputable travel authorities. Be aware of any political unrest, civil disturbances, or security concerns that may affect your travel plans.

Register with your embassy: If you're traveling to Petra from another country, consider registering with your embassy or consulate upon arrival in Jordan. This allows your government to contact you in case of an emergency and provide assistance if needed.

Stay informed about local laws and customs: Familiarize yourself with Jordanian laws, customs, and cultural norms to avoid inadvertently offending or disrespecting local traditions. Pay attention to dress codes, public behavior expectations, and prohibited activities, particularly in religious or conservative areas.

2.4.3. Health and Hygiene Practices:

Stay hydrated: Petra's climate can be hot and arid, especially during the summer months. Drink plenty of water throughout the day to stay hydrated and prevent dehydration, particularly if you're hiking or spending extended periods outdoors.

Protect yourself from the sun: Wear sunscreen with a high SPF, sunglasses, and a wide-brimmed hat to protect your skin and eyes from the sun's harmful rays. Seek shade during the hottest part of the day, typically between 10:00 AM and 4:00 PM.

Practice good hygiene: Wash your hands frequently with soap and water, especially before eating or after using the restroom. Carry hand sanitizer for situations where handwashing facilities are not readily available.

2.4.4. Safety in Petra:

Stay on designated trails: When exploring Petra's archaeological sites and hiking trails, stick to designated paths and follow signage and park regulations. Venturing off-trail can be dangerous and may pose risks such as falling rocks, uneven terrain, or encounters with wildlife.

Dress appropriately: Wear comfortable, sturdy footwear and lightweight, breathable clothing suitable for hiking and walking in hot weather.

Consider covering exposed skin to protect against sunburn and insect bites.

Be cautious around cliffs and steep terrain: Exercise caution when navigating cliffs, steep staircases, and narrow passageways in Petra, especially if you're prone to dizziness or have mobility limitations. Stay behind safety barriers and avoid leaning over ledges or edges.

2.4.5. Emergency Preparedness:

Carry essential supplies: Pack a small first aid kit with basic medical supplies such as adhesive bandages, antiseptic wipes, pain relievers, and any prescription medications you may need. Consider bringing a mobile phone with emergency contacts programmed and a portable charger.

Know emergency procedures: Familiarize yourself with emergency procedures and contact information for local emergency services, including medical facilities, police, and search and rescue teams. Keep a list of important phone numbers accessible in case of an emergency.

By following these comprehensive health and safety tips, you can minimize risks and maximize your enjoyment while exploring the ancient wonders of Petra. With proper preparation, awareness, and caution, your visit to Petra will be a memorable and enriching experience that leaves you with cherished memories for years to come.

2.5 Packing Essentials

Packing for a trip to Petra requires careful consideration of essential items to ensure comfort, safety, and convenience during your visit. Whether you're planning a day trip or an extended stay, here's an extensive list of packing essentials to help you prepare for your adventure:

2.5.1. Clothing:

Lightweight, breathable clothing: Opt for comfortable clothing suitable for warm weather, such as t-shirts, shorts, and lightweight pants or skirts. Avoid heavy fabrics that may cause overheating.

Sun protection: Pack a wide-brimmed hat, sunglasses, and sunscreen with a high SPF to protect your skin and eyes from the sun's harmful rays.

Layers: Although daytime temperatures in Petra can be hot, evenings and early mornings may be cooler. Bring a light jacket or sweater for layering to stay comfortable in changing weather conditions.

Sturdy footwear: Wear comfortable, closed-toe shoes with good traction for walking and hiking on uneven terrain. Avoid sandals or flip-flops that may not provide adequate support or protection.

Swimwear: If you plan to visit Petra's nearby attractions, such as the Dead Sea or Wadi Rum, pack swimwear and a towel for swimming or relaxing by the water.

2.5.2. Accessories:

Daypack or backpack: Carry a lightweight daypack or backpack to hold essential items such as water bottles, snacks, sunscreen, and a camera while exploring Petra.

Water bottle: Stay hydrated throughout the day by carrying a refillable water bottle. Consider bringing a hydration bladder or insulated bottle to keep water cool in the hot desert climate.

Portable charger: Keep your electronic devices powered up with a portable charger or power bank, especially if you plan to use your smartphone for navigation, photography, or communication.

Travel guide or map: Bring a guidebook, map, or smartphone app with information about Petra's attractions, hiking trails, and points of interest to help you navigate the site.

2.5.3. Health and Safety:

First aid kit: Pack a compact first aid kit with basic medical supplies such as adhesive bandages, antiseptic wipes, pain relievers, and any prescription medications you may need.

Hand sanitizer: Carry hand sanitizer or sanitizing wipes for quick and convenient hand hygiene, especially when handwashing facilities are not readily available.

Insect repellent: Protect yourself from mosquito bites and other insects by applying insect repellent containing DEET or other recommended ingredients.

Personal identification and emergency contact information: Carry a copy of your passport, travel insurance details, and emergency contact information in case of an emergency.

2.5.4. Miscellaneous Items:

Camera or smartphone: Capture memories of your visit to Petra with a camera or smartphone equipped with a quality camera. Don't forget to bring extra memory cards or storage space for photos and videos.

Snacks and refreshments: Pack snacks such as energy bars, nuts, fruits, or trail mix to keep you fueled and energized during your explorations. Consider bringing a picnic lunch or snacks for a midday break.

Travel journal or notebook: Record your thoughts, impressions, and experiences of Petra in a travel journal or notebook to preserve memories of your trip.

By packing these essential items, you'll be well-prepared to explore the wonders of Petra comfortably, safely, and conveniently. Remember to pack light, prioritize comfort, and tailor your packing list to suit your individual needs and preferences for a memorable and enjoyable visit to this ancient marvel.

3.0 Transportation

3.1 Getting to Petra

Getting to Petra, located in southern Jordan, involves several transportation options, each offering its own advantages in terms of convenience, cost, and travel experience. Here's an extensive guide to help you navigate the various transportation options and choose the best route for your journey to Petra:

3.1.1. By Air:

a. Queen Alia International Airport (AMM): Jordan's main international airport, located near the capital city of Amman, is the primary gateway for travelers arriving by air. From Queen Alia International Airport, visitors can reach Petra via the following options:

Domestic Flights: While there are no airports in close proximity to Petra, domestic flights from Amman to nearby cities such as Aqaba or Eilat in Israel are available. From there, travelers can continue their journey to Petra by land.

b. King Hussein International Airport (AQJ): Located in Aqaba, King Hussein International Airport serves as an alternative entry point for travelers arriving by air. From Aqaba, visitors can reach Petra by road, approximately a 2.5 to 3-hour drive.

3.1.2. By Land:

a. Private Transfer: One of the most convenient and comfortable ways to reach Petra is by arranging a private transfer from major cities such as Amman or Aqaba. Private transfers offer door-to-door service and can be customized to suit your schedule and preferences.

b. Rental Car: Renting a car provides flexibility and independence for travelers exploring Jordan. From Amman or Aqaba, visitors can drive to Petra via well-maintained highways and scenic routes. It's advisable to obtain an International Driving Permit (IDP) and familiarize yourself with local traffic regulations before driving in Jordan.

c. Public Bus: Several bus companies operate routes between major cities and tourist destinations in Jordan, including Petra. The JETT bus company offers daily bus services from Amman to Petra, with multiple departures throughout the day. The journey takes approximately 3.5 to 4 hours and offers an affordable transportation option for budget-conscious travelers.

d. Shared Taxi (Service Taxi): Shared taxis, known as "service taxis" or "sheruts," are a common mode of transportation in Jordan. Travelers can find shared taxis departing from Amman or Aqaba to Petra from designated taxi stations or transportation hubs. Shared taxis may be more flexible in terms of departure times but can be crowded and less comfortable than private transfers.

3.1.3. By Guided Tour:

Many tour operators offer guided tours to Petra from various cities in Jordan, as well as neighboring countries such as Israel and Egypt. Guided tours provide a hassle-free and informative travel experience, with transportation, accommodation, and guided sightseeing included in the package. Travelers can choose from day tours, multi-day tours, or customized itineraries tailored to their preferences.

3.1.4. By Camel or Horseback:

For a unique and memorable experience, adventurous travelers can opt to reach Petra by camel or horseback. Guided camel or horseback tours are available from nearby towns and Bedouin camps, offering an alternative mode of transportation and a chance to experience the desert landscape in a traditional manner.

Regardless of the transportation option you choose, reaching Petra is a rewarding journey filled with anticipation and excitement. Whether you prefer the convenience of a private transfer, the flexibility of a rental car, or the adventure of a guided tour, there are plenty of options available to suit your travel style and preferences. By planning ahead and considering factors such as budget, time constraints, and personal comfort, you can make the most of your journey to Petra and create unforgettable memories along the way.

3.2 Getting Around Petra

Once you've arrived at Petra, navigating the expansive archaeological site and its surrounding areas requires careful planning and consideration of transportation options. Here's an extensive guide to help you get around Petra efficiently and comfortably:

3.2.1. Walking:

a. Main Entrance to the Siq: The journey into Petra begins with a walk through the Siq, a narrow canyon that serves as the main entrance to the archaeological site. Walking through the Siq allows visitors to experience the dramatic natural beauty of the canyon and marvel at the towering sandstone cliffs.

b. Exploring the Main Sites: Many of Petra's main attractions, including the Treasury (Al-Khazneh), the Street of Facades, and the Royal Tombs, are accessible on foot from the main entrance. Walking paths and trails lead visitors through the ancient city, providing opportunities to admire the intricate rock-cut architecture and historical landmarks up close.

c. Hiking Trails: For adventurous travelers, Petra offers several hiking trails that lead to lesser-known sites and panoramic viewpoints. Popular hiking routes include the trail to the Monastery (Ad Deir) and the High Place of Sacrifice, both of which offer stunning views of Petra's rugged landscape.

3.2.2. Horseback Riding:

a. Horse Carriages: For visitors who prefer not to walk the entire distance from the main entrance to the Treasury, horse-drawn carriages are available for hire. These horse-drawn carriages offer a convenient and scenic mode of transportation, allowing passengers to relax and enjoy the journey through the Siq.

b. Horseback Riding: Guided horseback riding tours are also available for those who wish to explore Petra on horseback. Experienced local guides lead visitors on horseback through the archaeological site, providing insight into Petra's history and culture along the way.

3.2.3. Camel Rides:

For a truly memorable experience, travelers can opt for camel rides within Petra. Guided camel tours offer a unique perspective of the ancient city, allowing riders to traverse the rugged terrain and capture panoramic views of Petra's iconic monuments.

3.2.4. Donkey Rides:

Donkey rides are another transportation option available for visitors exploring Petra. Donkeys can be hired to transport passengers along designated routes within the archaeological site, providing an alternative mode of transportation for those who prefer not to walk long distances.

3.2.5. Guided Tours:

For a comprehensive exploration of Petra's highlights and hidden gems, guided tours led by knowledgeable local guides are an excellent option. Guided tours offer insight into Petra's history, architecture, and significance, allowing visitors to gain a deeper understanding of this ancient wonder.

3.2.6. Self-Guided Exploration:

For independent travelers who prefer to explore Petra at their own pace, self-guided exploration is a viable option. Armed with a map, guidebook, or smartphone app, visitors can navigate the archaeological site independently, stopping to admire landmarks, take photographs, and soak in the atmosphere at their leisure.

Getting around Petra offers a variety of transportation options to suit every traveler's preferences and mobility needs. Whether you choose to explore on foot, by horseback, or with the assistance of a local guide, navigating Petra's ancient wonders is an unforgettable journey filled with discovery, adventure, and awe-inspiring beauty. By planning ahead and considering your transportation preferences, you can make the most of your visit to this iconic archaeological site and create lasting memories of your time in Petra.

3.3 Public Transportation

Public transportation in Jordan provides an affordable and convenient way for residents and visitors alike to travel between cities, towns, and tourist destinations across the country. While the public transportation network may not be as extensive as in some other countries, it offers several options for getting around, including buses, minibusses (service taxis), and trains. Here's an extensive guide to public transportation in Jordan:

3.3.1. Buses:

a. JETT Bus Company: The JETT (Jordan Express Tourist Transportation) Bus Company operates a network of intercity buses connecting major cities and tourist destinations in Jordan. JETT buses are modern, air-conditioned coaches equipped with comfortable seating and onboard amenities such as Wi-Fi and restrooms. They offer regular services between Amman, Petra, Aqaba, Jerash, and other popular destinations, making them a popular choice for travelers seeking reliable and comfortable transportation.

b. Local Buses: In addition to intercity buses, Jordan's cities and towns are served by local bus networks operated by various public and private companies. Local buses provide affordable transportation within urban areas and between neighboring towns, catering primarily to residents commuting to work, school, or shopping centers. While local buses may not offer the same level of comfort or amenities as intercity buses, they are a budget-friendly option for getting around Jordan's cities and towns.

3.3.2. Minibusses (Service Taxis):

Minibusses, known locally as "service taxis" or "sheruts," are a common mode of transportation in Jordan, especially for shorter distances and routes not served by larger buses. These shared taxis operate on fixed routes and pick up passengers at designated stops along the way. Service taxis are often faster and more flexible than buses, making them a convenient option for travelers navigating urban areas or traveling between towns. However, they can be crowded and may not adhere to strict schedules, so it's advisable to confirm the route and fare with the driver before boarding.

3.3.3. Trains:

Jordan's railway network is relatively limited compared to other forms of public transportation, with only one operational passenger train route currently in service. The Hijaz Railway, operated by the Jordan Hejaz Railway Corporation, runs between Amman and the town of Rusayfah, approximately 30 kilometers south of the capital. The railway primarily serves commuters traveling between Amman and Rusayfah for work or school, with limited amenities and frequency of service. While the Hijaz Railway may not be a practical option for most travelers, it offers a unique opportunity to experience Jordan's railway heritage and scenic countryside.

3.3.4. Taxi Services:

Taxis are readily available in urban areas and tourist destinations throughout Jordan, offering on-demand transportation for short distances or door-to-door service. Both metered taxis and private hire taxis (known as "service taxis") are available, with fares typically negotiated with the driver before the journey begins. While taxis may be more expensive than buses or minibusses, they offer convenience and flexibility, especially for travelers with limited mobility or specific transportation needs.

3.3.5. Car Rental:

For travelers seeking flexibility and independence, car rental is a popular option for exploring Jordan's cities, towns, and scenic landscapes. Several international and local car rental companies operate in Jordan, offering a range of vehicles to suit different budgets and preferences. Renting a car allows travelers to explore at their own pace, venture off the beaten path, and access remote destinations not served by public transportation. However, it's important to familiarize yourself with local traffic regulations, road conditions, and driving customs before embarking on a road trip in Jordan.

Public transportation in Jordan offers a range of options for getting around the country, from intercity buses and minibusses to trains and taxis. Whether you're traveling between major cities, exploring urban areas, or visiting tourist attractions like Petra and the Dead Sea, there's a transportation option to suit every traveler's needs and preferences. By planning ahead, familiarizing yourself with the available transportation options, and considering factors such as cost, comfort, and convenience, you can navigate Jordan's public transportation network with ease and enjoy a memorable journey through this fascinating country.

4.0 Accommodation

4.1 Luxury hotel

Jordan is home to a selection of luxury hotels that offer world-class amenities, impeccable service, and breathtaking settings for travelers seeking the ultimate in comfort and indulgence. From opulent resorts overlooking the Dead Sea to boutique hotels nestled in historic cities, here's an extensive overview of some of the top luxury accommodations in Jordan:

4.1.1. Kempinski Hotel Ishtar Dead Sea:

Location: Sweimeh, Dead Sea

Description: Nestled along the shores of the Dead Sea, the Kempinski Hotel Ishtar is a five-star luxury resort renowned for its stunning architecture, lush gardens, and panoramic views of the lowest point on Earth. The hotel features a range of luxurious accommodations, including spacious rooms, suites, and private villas, each elegantly appointed with modern amenities and stylish décor. Guests can indulge in a variety of dining options, including Mediterranean cuisine, Middle Eastern specialties, and international fare, served in exquisite settings overlooking the Dead Sea. The hotel also offers a state-of-the-art spa and wellness center, infinity pools, private beach access, and a range of recreational activities, making it the perfect destination for a relaxing and rejuvenating getaway.

4.1.2. Four Seasons Hotel Amman:

Location: Amman

Description: Situated in the heart of Jordan's capital city, the Four Seasons Hotel Amman offers unparalleled luxury and sophistication for discerning travelers. The hotel's elegant rooms and suites feature contemporary design, plush furnishings, and panoramic views of the city skyline. Guests can enjoy a variety of dining options, including authentic Jordanian cuisine, international specialties, and innovative cocktails, served in stylish restaurants and lounges. The hotel also boasts a world-class spa and wellness center, fitness facilities, rooftop pool, and personalized concierge services, ensuring an unforgettable stay in Amman.

4.1.3. Movenpick Resort & Spa Dead Sea:

Location: Sweimeh, Dead Sea

Description: Set amidst lush gardens overlooking the Dead Sea, the Movenpick Resort & Spa offers a luxurious retreat for travelers seeking relaxation and rejuvenation. The hotel's spacious rooms and suites feature modern amenities, elegant furnishings, and private balconies with stunning views of the Dead Sea landscape. Guests can indulge in a variety of dining experiences, including international buffets, Mediterranean cuisine, and seafood specialties, served in stylish restaurants and outdoor terraces. The hotel's award-winning Zara Spa offers a range of holistic treatments, therapeutic pools, and relaxation areas, providing the perfect escape from the stresses of everyday life.

4.1.4. The St. Regis Amman:

Location: Amman

Description: Situated in the prestigious Abdoun neighborhood of Amman, The St. Regis Amman is a luxury hotel renowned for its timeless elegance, impeccable service, and sophisticated ambiance. The hotel's spacious rooms and suites feature luxurious furnishings, state-of-the-art technology, and panoramic views of the city skyline. Guests can dine in style at the hotel's signature restaurants, enjoy afternoon tea in the elegant tea lounge, or unwind with cocktails and live music in the chic bar and lounge. The hotel also offers a range of amenities, including a rooftop pool, fitness center, spa, and personalized butler service, ensuring a truly luxurious and memorable stay in Amman.

4.1.5. Ma'In Hot Springs Resort & Spa:

Location: Ma'In, Dead Sea

Description: Tucked away in a tranquil oasis amidst the dramatic landscapes of Ma'In, the Ma'In Hot Springs Resort & Spa offers a unique blend of luxury, wellness, and natural beauty. The resort's elegant accommodations include luxurious rooms, suites, and villas, each featuring private balconies with panoramic views of the surrounding mountains and hot springs. Guests can indulge in a variety of wellness experiences, including thermal hot spring baths, rejuvenating spa treatments, and holistic wellness programs, designed to promote relaxation and rejuvenation. The resort also offers gourmet dining options, outdoor pools, hiking trails, and cultural activities, providing a truly immersive and unforgettable experience in the heart of Jordan.

Jordan's luxury hotels offer a haven of comfort, elegance, and unparalleled hospitality for travelers seeking an indulgent escape. Whether you're relaxing by the Dead Sea, exploring the historic streets of Amman, or immersing yourself in the natural beauty of Ma'In, these exquisite accommodations provide the perfect setting for an unforgettable luxury getaway in Jordan.

4.2 Budget-Friendly Options

For travelers exploring Jordan on a budget, there are numerous affordable accommodation options available across the country, ranging from budget hotels and guesthouses to hostels and campgrounds. Here's an extensive overview of some of the best budget-friendly accommodation options in Jordan:

4.2.1. Budget Hotels and Guesthouses:

a. Amman Palace Hotel (Amman):

Located in the heart of Amman's downtown area, the Amman Palace Hotel offers budget-friendly accommodation with comfortable rooms, modern amenities, and a convenient location near major attractions, restaurants, and shops.

b. Petra Moon Hotel (Petra): Situated within walking distance of the entrance to Petra, the Petra Moon Hotel provides affordable rooms and suites with stunning views of the surrounding mountains. Guests can enjoy complimentary breakfast, Wi-Fi, and easy access to Petra's archaeological wonders.

c. Nomads Hotel (Wadi Musa):

Perfect for budget travelers and backpackers, Nomads Hotel offers affordable dormitory-style accommodation and private rooms with shared bathrooms. The hotel features a communal kitchen, rooftop terrace, and friendly staff who can assist with travel arrangements and sightseeing tours.

4.2.2. Hostels:

a. Jordan Tower Hotel (Amman):

This popular hostel in Amman's downtown area offers dormitory beds and private rooms at budget-friendly prices. Guests can enjoy a complimentary breakfast, free Wi-Fi, and a lively atmosphere with fellow travelers from around the world.

b. Petra Gate Hostel (Petra): Conveniently located near the entrance to Petra, Petra Gate Hostel offers affordable dormitory beds and private rooms with basic amenities. The hostel features a communal kitchen, rooftop terrace, and friendly staff who can provide tips and recommendations for exploring Petra.

c. Cliff Hostel (Wadi Rum):

For travelers visiting the stunning desert landscapes of Wadi Rum, Cliff Hostel offers affordable accommodation in traditional Bedouin-style tents and rooms. Guests can enjoy guided tours, camel rides, and cultural experiences organized by the hostel's friendly staff.

4.2.3. Camping:

a. Dana Biosphere Reserve (Dana): Nature-loving travelers can camp under the stars in the Dana Biosphere Reserve, Jordan's largest nature reserve. The reserve offers designated camping areas with basic facilities, stunning views, and opportunities for hiking, birdwatching, and stargazing.

b. Wadi Rum Desert Camps (Wadi Rum): Experience the magic of the desert by camping in Wadi Rum, where numerous desert camps offer affordable accommodation in traditional Bedouin tents. Guests can enjoy campfire dinners, Bedouin hospitality, and guided tours of the desert's iconic landmarks.

4.2.4. Homestays:

a. Local Homestays (Various Locations): For an authentic cultural experience, consider staying with a local family in Jordan. Many families offer affordable homestay accommodation, where guests can enjoy home-cooked meals, cultural exchanges, and insights into Jordanian life and traditions.

b. Airbnb: Airbnb offers a wide range of budget-friendly accommodation options in Jordan, including private rooms, apartments, and guesthouses hosted by local residents. Guests can often find affordable rates, especially for longer stays, and enjoy the convenience of self-catering facilities and personalized experiences.

Traveling on a budget in Jordan doesn't mean sacrificing comfort or convenience. With a wide range of affordable accommodation options available, thrifty travelers can explore Jordan's rich history, stunning landscapes, and vibrant culture without breaking the bank. Whether you prefer budget hotels, hostels, camping, or homestays, there's something to suit every traveler's budget and preferences in Jordan.

4.3 Airbnb and Vacation Rentals

Airbnb and vacation rentals offer travelers a unique and personalized alternative to traditional hotels, providing a wide range of accommodation options in Jordan's cities, towns, and tourist destinations. From cozy apartments in urban neighborhoods to luxurious villas overlooking the Dead Sea, here's an extensive overview of Airbnb and vacation rentals in Jordan:

4.3.1. Apartments:

a. Urban Apartments (Amman): Airbnb offers a variety of apartments in Amman, Jordan's capital city, ranging from cozy studios to spacious penthouses. Travelers can choose from apartments located in vibrant neighborhoods such as Rainbow Street, Abdoun, and Jabal Amman, offering easy access to restaurants, cafes, shops, and cultural attractions.

b. Coastal Apartments (Aqaba): For travelers visiting the Red Sea resort city of Aqaba, Airbnb offers a selection of beachfront apartments and condos with stunning views of the Red Sea. Guests can enjoy amenities such as swimming pools, private balconies, and easy access to

Aqaba's beaches, dive sites, and water sports activities.

4.3.2. Villas and Vacation Homes:

a. Dead Sea Villas: Experience luxury living at the Dead Sea with Airbnb's selection of villas and vacation homes overlooking the tranquil waters of the world's lowest point. These spacious properties feature private pools, lush gardens, and panoramic views of the Dead Sea landscape, providing the perfect setting for a relaxing retreat.

b. Wadi Rum Desert Camps: For an unforgettable desert experience, Airbnb offers a range of desert camps and Bedouin-style tents in Wadi Rum. Guests can immerse themselves in the beauty of the desert, enjoy traditional Bedouin hospitality, and explore the stunning landscapes of Wadi Rum on guided tours and camel rides organized by their hosts.

4.3.3. Traditional Guesthouses:

a. Petra Guesthouses: Travelers visiting the ancient city of Petra can find charming guesthouses and bed and breakfast accommodations on Airbnb, offering cozy rooms, home-cooked meals, and personalized service. Many guesthouses are located within walking distance of Petra's archaeological site, making them an ideal base for exploring the iconic monuments and hiking trails.

b. Historic Homes (Jerash): Immerse yourself in Jordan's rich history by staying in a traditional guesthouse or historic home in Jerash, home to one of the best-preserved Roman cities in the world. Airbnb offers a selection of charming properties with authentic architecture, antique furnishings, and modern amenities, allowing guests to experience the charm of Jordan's past while enjoying modern comforts.

4.3.4. Budget-Friendly Options:

a. Shared Accommodations: For budget-conscious travelers, Airbnb offers shared accommodations such as private rooms or shared dormitories in Jordan's cities and tourist destinations. Shared accommodations provide an affordable option for solo travelers or those looking to meet fellow travelers and locals.

b. Rural Retreats: Escape the hustle and bustle of city life with Airbnb's selection of rural retreats and countryside cottages in Jordan's scenic countryside. Guests can unwind in peaceful surroundings, enjoy fresh air, and explore the natural beauty and cultural heritage of rural Jordan.

Airbnb and vacation rentals offer travelers a diverse array of accommodation options in Jordan, ranging from urban apartments and beachfront condos to desert camps and historic guesthouses. Whether you're seeking luxury and comfort or authenticity and adventure, Airbnb has something to suit every traveler's needs and preferences in Jordan. With personalized experiences, local insights, and competitive pricing, Airbnb and vacation rentals provide a unique opportunity to immerse yourself in Jordanian culture, hospitality, and landscapes while enjoying the comforts of home away from home.

4.4 Hostels

Hostels provide budget-conscious travelers with affordable accommodation options, social atmospheres, and unique experiences in Jordan's cities, towns, and tourist destinations. Offering dormitory beds, private rooms, communal spaces, and organized activities, hostels cater to a diverse range of travelers seeking affordability, convenience, and opportunities for social interaction. Here's an extensive overview of hostels in Jordan:

4.4.1. Hostel Types:

a. Traditional Hostels: Traditional hostels in Jordan typically offer dormitory-style accommodation with shared bathrooms and communal areas. Dormitory rooms may range from small dorms with four to six beds to larger dorms with 10 or more beds, providing options for solo travelers, backpackers, and groups.

b. Boutique Hostels: Some hostels in Jordan offer boutique-style accommodation with a focus on design, comfort, and personalized service. Boutique hostels may feature stylish interiors, private rooms with ensuite bathrooms, and amenities such as rooftop terraces, social lounges, and on-site cafes or bars.

c. Eco-Friendly Hostels: As eco-tourism becomes increasingly popular in Jordan, eco-friendly hostels are emerging as sustainable accommodation options for environmentally-conscious travelers. These hostels may incorporate eco-friendly practices such as recycling, energy conservation, and organic gardening, providing eco-conscious travelers with a responsible and ethical lodging choice.

4.4.2. Amenities and Facilities:

a. Dormitory Rooms: Hostels typically offer dormitory rooms with bunk beds or single beds, providing affordable accommodation for budget travelers. Dormitory rooms may be mixed-gender or single-gender, and guests usually have access to lockers or storage facilities for their belongings.

b. Private Rooms: In addition to dormitory beds, many hostels offer private rooms with ensuite or shared bathrooms for travelers seeking more privacy and comfort. Private rooms may be available in various configurations, including single, double, twin, or family rooms, catering to different traveler preferences and group sizes.

c. Common Areas: Hostels feature communal areas such as lounges, kitchens, dining areas, and outdoor spaces where guests can socialize, relax, and interact with fellow travelers. Common areas may include amenities such as board games, books, TV screens, and Wi-Fi access, providing opportunities for socializing and entertainment.

d. Organized Activities: Some hostels organize social activities, cultural events, and guided tours to help guests explore Jordan's attractions, meet other travelers, and immerse themselves in local culture. Activities may include city tours, cooking classes, language exchanges, and outdoor adventures, enhancing the hostel experience and creating memorable moments for guests.

4.4.3. Locations:

a. Urban Hostels: Hostels in Jordan's cities, such as Amman, Petra, and Aqaba, are centrally located near major attractions, public transportation hubs, restaurants, and nightlife venues. Urban hostels offer easy access to cultural landmarks, shopping districts, and entertainment options, making them ideal bases for exploring city highlights.

b. Rural Hostels: In rural areas and natural reserves such as Dana Biosphere Reserve and Wadi Rum, hostels provide accommodation for travelers seeking outdoor adventures, eco-tourism experiences, and wilderness escapes. Rural hostels offer opportunities for hiking, wildlife watching, stargazing, and cultural encounters with local communities, providing a unique and immersive travel experience.

4.4.4. Benefits of Staying in Hostels:

a. Affordability: Hostels offer budget-friendly accommodation options for travelers seeking to minimize lodging expenses and allocate more funds for activities, dining, and sightseeing.

b. Social Atmosphere: Hostels provide opportunities for social interaction, cultural exchange, and friendship-building among guests from diverse backgrounds and nationalities.

c. Convenience: Hostels often offer amenities such as 24-hour reception, luggage storage, laundry facilities, and travel desk services to enhance guest convenience and comfort.

d. Flexibility: Hostels accommodate various travel styles and preferences, including solo travel, group travel, backpacking, and budget travel, catering to a wide range of traveler needs and interests.

Hostels in Jordan offer affordable, social, and convenient accommodation options for budget-conscious travelers seeking unique and immersive travel experiences. With a variety of hostel types, amenities, locations, and organized activities, hostels cater to diverse traveler preferences and provide opportunities for cultural exchange, adventure, and friendship-building. Whether you're exploring Jordan's cities, natural wonders, or cultural heritage sites, staying in a hostel offers a memorable and rewarding travel experience that's both affordable and enriching.

5.0 Shopping Guide

5.1 Shopping mall

Shopping malls in Jordan offer visitors a comprehensive retail experience, combining a diverse selection of stores, restaurants, entertainment venues, and leisure facilities under one roof. From upscale boutiques and international brands to local artisans and specialty shops, Jordan's shopping malls cater to a wide range of tastes, preferences, and budgets. Here's an extensive overview of shopping malls in Jordan:

5.1.1. City Mall (Amman):

Location: Al Rabiyah, Amman

Description: City Mall is one of Jordan's largest and most popular shopping destinations, featuring over 200 stores, restaurants, and entertainment venues spread across multiple levels. The mall offers a diverse mix of international and local brands, including fashion retailers, electronics stores, beauty boutiques, and department stores. Visitors can enjoy a wide range of dining options, from fast-food chains to fine-dining restaurants, as well as entertainment facilities such as a multiplex cinema, indoor amusement park, and family entertainment center.

5.1.2. Taj Mall (Amman):

Location: Abdoun, Amman

Description: Taj Mall is a premier shopping destination located in the upscale Abdoun neighborhood of Amman, offering a sophisticated retail experience with a focus on luxury brands and designer boutiques. The mall features a curated selection of high-end fashion labels, jewelry stores, beauty salons, and lifestyle retailers, as well as gourmet restaurants, cafes, and dessert parlors. Visitors can indulge in upscale shopping, dining, and leisure activities in an elegant and upscale environment.

5.1.3. Mecca Mall (Amman):

Location: Swaifyeh, Amman
Description: Mecca Mall is a popular shopping and entertainment complex located in the Swaifyeh district of Amman, offering a diverse range of retail, dining, and leisure options for visitors of all ages. The mall boasts a large

hypermarket, department stores, fashion retailers, home furnishing stores, and specialty shops, as well as a food court, international restaurants, and cafes. Entertainment facilities at Mecca Mall include a multiplex cinema, arcade games, children's play areas, and a bowling alley, providing entertainment for the whole family.

5.1.4. Abdali Mall (Amman):

Location: Abdali, Amman

Description: Abdali Mall is a modern shopping and lifestyle destination located in the heart of Amman's Abdali district, offering a contemporary retail experience with a focus on fashion, dining, and entertainment. The mall features a diverse mix of international and local brands, including fashion retailers, electronics stores, bookshops, and specialty boutiques. Visitors can dine at a variety of restaurants and cafes, enjoy leisure activities such as a multiplex cinema and children's entertainment center, and explore the mall's stylish and modern architecture.

5.1.5. Galleria Mall (Amman):

Location: Sweifieh, Amman
Description: Galleria Mall is a boutique shopping destination located in the Sweifieh district of Amman, offering a curated selection

of upscale fashion brands, designer boutiques, and specialty stores. The mall features stylish and contemporary architecture, with a focus on luxury shopping, gourmet dining, and cultural experiences. Visitors can explore high-end fashion labels, jewelry stores, beauty salons, and art galleries, as well as enjoy fine-dining restaurants, cafes, and wine bars in an elegant and sophisticated setting.

5.1.6. The Boulevard (Amman):

Location: Abdali, Amman

Description: The Boulevard is a mixed-use development located in Amman's Abdali district, comprising a shopping mall, office towers, residential apartments, and a hotel. The mall features a diverse mix of retail, dining, and entertainment options, including fashion boutiques, international brands, cafes, restaurants, and a food court. Visitors can also enjoy outdoor spaces, landscaped gardens, and cultural events at The Boulevard, making it a popular destination for shopping, dining, and leisure activities in Amman.

Shopping malls in Jordan offer visitors a modern, convenient, and comprehensive retail experience, with a diverse range of stores, restaurants, entertainment venues, and leisure facilities to suit every taste and preference. Whether you're looking for upscale fashion, gourmet dining, family-friendly entertainment, or cultural experiences, Jordan's shopping malls provide a vibrant and dynamic environment for shopping, dining, and socializing with friends and family. With their convenient locations, extensive amenities, and diverse offerings, shopping malls in Jordan are not just retail destinations but vibrant hubs of activity and community life.

5.2 Local Markets

Local markets, known as "souqs" in Arabic, are an integral part of Jordanian culture and daily life, offering visitors a glimpse into the country's rich heritage, traditional crafts, and bustling commerce. From bustling bazaars in ancient cities to vibrant street markets in modern neighborhoods, Jordan's local markets are vibrant hubs of activity, where locals and tourists alike come together to shop, socialize, and experience the sights, sounds, and flavors of Jordan. Here's an extensive overview of local markets in Jordan:

5.2.1. Downtown Souq (Amman):

Location: Downtown Amman (Al Balad)

Description: Downtown Amman is home to one of Jordan's oldest and most vibrant markets, where narrow alleyways and bustling streets are lined with shops, stalls, and vendors selling a wide variety of goods, including clothing, accessories, spices, traditional handicrafts, and souvenirs. Visitors can explore the maze-like streets of the souq, haggle with vendors, and sample local delicacies such as falafel, shawarma, and freshly squeezed juice. The Downtown Souq is also home to historical landmarks such as the Roman Theater, Al-Husseini Mosque, and Rainbow Street, adding to its charm and appeal as a cultural and commercial hub in the heart of Amman.

5.2.2. Souq Al-Salt (Salt):

Location: Salt

Description: Souq Al-Salt is a historic market in the city of Salt, located northwest of Amman, known for its traditional architecture, lively atmosphere, and diverse array of goods. The souq features narrow alleys lined with shops selling textiles, spices, handicrafts, antiques, and local products such as olive oil, soap, and sweets. Visitors can explore the historic buildings, interact with friendly locals, and discover hidden treasures while wandering through the maze-like streets of Souq Al-Salt.

5.2.3. Souq Jara (Amman):

Location: Jabal Amman, Amman
Description: Souq Jara is a popular open-air market held every Friday in Amman's Jabal Amman neighborhood, offering a lively mix of vendors, artisans, musicians, and street performers. The market features stalls selling handmade crafts, jewelry, clothing, accessories, and vintage items, as well as food vendors offering traditional Jordanian snacks and beverages. Souq Jara also hosts live music performances, cultural events, and art exhibitions, creating a festive and vibrant atmosphere that attracts locals and tourists alike.

5.2.4. Souq Al-Bukharia (Aqaba):

Location: Aqaba

Description: Souq Al-Bukharia is a bustling market located in the heart of Aqaba's old town, offering visitors a glimpse into the city's maritime history, Bedouin culture, and vibrant trade scene. The market features a variety of shops and stalls selling everything from spices, herbs, and textiles to jewelry, handicrafts, and souvenirs. Visitors can wander through the narrow alleyways, interact with local vendors, and sample traditional Jordanian dishes at the market's many restaurants and cafes.

5.2.5. Souq Al-Hamidiyya (Jerash):

Location: Jerash

Description: Souq Al-Hamidiyya is a traditional market located near the ancient ruins of Jerash, offering visitors a unique shopping experience amidst Roman ruins and historic landmarks. The market features shops selling local handicrafts, ceramics, textiles, and souvenirs, as well as vendors offering fresh produce, spices, and traditional Jordanian products. Visitors can explore the market's winding streets, admire the architecture, and soak in the atmosphere of this historic trading hub.

Local markets in Jordan are vibrant, colorful, and dynamic spaces that reflect the country's rich cultural heritage, entrepreneurial spirit, and sense of community. Whether you're shopping for souvenirs, sampling local cuisine, or simply soaking in the sights and sounds of Jordanian life, a visit to a local market is an essential part of any travel experience in Jordan. With their diverse offerings, lively atmosphere, and authentic charm, Jordan's local markets provide a window into the country's past, present, and future, making them a must-visit destination for travelers seeking to explore the heart and soul of Jordan.

5.3 Unique Souvenirs

Bringing home souvenirs from your travels in Jordan allows you to cherish memories of your experiences while also supporting local artisans and businesses. Jordan offers a rich beauty of cultural heritage, traditional crafts, and distinctive products that make for unique and meaningful souvenirs. From handmade crafts and culinary delights to archaeological replicas and cultural artifacts, here's an extensive guide to unique souvenirs from Jordan:

5.3.1. Handcrafted Pottery:
Jordan has a long tradition of pottery-making, with artisans producing a wide range of pottery items such as vases, bowls, plates, and decorative pieces. Look for pottery in traditional Jordanian designs and motifs, often featuring

intricate patterns and vibrant colors inspired by nature and history.

5.3.2. Palestinian Embroidery:

Traditional Palestinian embroidery, known as "tatreez," is a cherished craft in Jordan, passed down through generations of Palestinian and Jordanian women. Look for hand-embroidered textiles such as scarves, shawls, pillow covers, and bags, featuring intricate patterns and vibrant colors that reflect Palestinian heritage and cultural identity.

5.3.3. Dead Sea Products:
The Dead Sea is renowned for its therapeutic properties, and products made from Dead Sea

minerals are popular souvenirs for visitors to Jordan. Look for Dead Sea skincare products such as mud masks, bath salts, and lotions, prized for their rejuvenating and healing effects on the skin.

5.3.4. Arabic Calligraphy Art:

Arabic calligraphy is an ancient art form that holds deep cultural and religious significance in Jordan and the wider Arab world. Look for handcrafted calligraphy artwork featuring verses from the Quran, proverbs, or personal names, beautifully rendered in intricate Arabic script.

5.3.5. Bedouin Jewelry:

Bedouin jewelry reflects the nomadic heritage of Jordan's Bedouin tribes, featuring bold designs, intricate patterns, and vibrant colors. Look for handmade jewelry pieces such as necklaces, bracelets, earrings, and rings, crafted from silver, semi-precious stones, and colorful beads, often incorporating traditional symbols and motifs.

5.3.6. Olive Wood Crafts:

Jordan is known for its olive trees, and artisans transform olive wood into a variety of handmade crafts such as cutting boards, utensils, figurines, and religious icons. Look for olive wood products with intricate carvings and natural wood grain patterns, showcasing the beauty and durability of this sustainable material.

5.3.7. Arabic Coffee Pots (Dallah):

The traditional Arabic coffee pot, known as "dallah" or "ibrik," is a symbol of hospitality and cultural heritage in Jordan. Look for decorative dallahs made from brass, copper, or silver, featuring intricate designs and patterns inspired by Jordanian and Middle Eastern motifs.

5.3.8. Mosaic Art:
Jordan has a rich tradition of mosaic art, dating back to ancient times, with intricate mosaics adorning archaeological sites, churches, and mosques throughout the country. Look for mosaic-inspired souvenirs such as coasters, trivets, trays, and decorative tiles, showcasing the vibrant colors and geometric patterns of Jordanian mosaic design.

5.3.9. Arabic Sweets and Spices:
Jordanian cuisine is known for its rich flavors and aromatic spices, and local sweets and spices make for delicious and unique souvenirs. Look for traditional Jordanian sweets such as baklava, knafeh, and ma'amoul, as well as spices such as za'atar, sumac, and baharat, packaged in decorative tins or jars.

Souvenir shopping in Jordan offers a delightful opportunity to discover the country's rich cultural heritage, traditional crafts, and culinary delights. Whether you're exploring local markets, artisan workshops, or boutique stores, you'll find an array of unique and meaningful souvenirs to commemorate your journey and share the beauty and craftsmanship of Jordan with friends and family back home. From handcrafted pottery and Palestinian embroidery to Dead Sea products and Arabic calligraphy art, each souvenir tells a story and preserves a piece of Jordan's rich cultural beauty for generations to come.

6.0 Cuisine and Dining

6.1 Local Petra Dishes

Petra, nestled in the heart of Jordan's desert landscape, offers not only breathtaking archaeological wonders but also a rich culinary heritage influenced by the region's diverse cultural traditions. Exploring the local cuisine of Petra is an essential part of immersing oneself in the vibrant beautyof Jordanian culture. From hearty stews and grilled meats to aromatic spices and freshly baked bread, here's an extensive guide to the local dishes you must savor while visiting Petra:

6.1.1. Mansaf:

Mansaf is Jordan's national dish and a quintessential part of Bedouin cuisine. It consists of tender lamb cooked in a yogurt-based sauce, flavored with spices such as cardamom, turmeric, and cumin. The dish is typically served on a bed of rice and garnished with toasted almonds and pine nuts, creating a rich and savory flavor profile that reflects the hospitality and generosity of Jordanian culture.

6.1.2. Zarb:

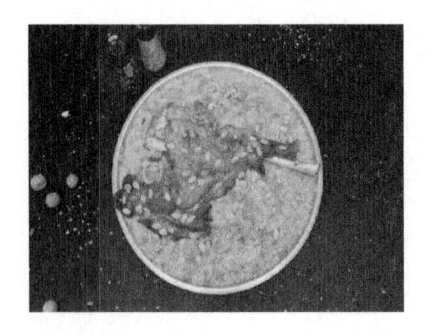

Zarb is a traditional Bedouin feast cooked in an underground oven, known as a "taboon," which consists of layers of meat, vegetables, and rice wrapped in palm leaves and buried in hot coals. The slow-cooking process infuses the ingredients with smoky flavors, resulting in tender and aromatic dishes. Zarb is often served at special occasions and gatherings, showcasing the communal spirit and culinary traditions of the Bedouin people.

6.1.3. Maglouba:

Maglouba, which translates to "upside-down" in Arabic, is a flavorful one-pot dish made with layers of rice, vegetables, and meat, such as chicken or lamb, cooked together and then flipped upside down before serving. The dish is seasoned with spices such as cinnamon, allspice, and cloves, imparting a fragrant and aromatic aroma. Maglouba is a comforting and hearty meal that is enjoyed by locals and visitors alike.

6.1.4. Jordanian Mezze:

Jordanian mezze offers a delightful array of small dishes and appetizers that showcase the diverse flavors and ingredients of Jordanian cuisine. Mezze may include dishes such as hummus (chickpea dip), baba ghanoush (eggplant dip), tabbouleh (parsley salad), falafel (fried chickpea balls), and muhammara (red pepper and walnut dip), served with fresh bread or pita for dipping.

6.1.5. Sfiha:

Sfiha, also known as "Arabic pizza," is a popular street food in Jordan made with a thin crust topped with minced meat, onions, tomatoes, and spices, then baked to perfection. Sfiha is often enjoyed as a quick and savory snack, served hot and fresh from local bakeries and street vendors in Petra and throughout Jordan.

6.1.6. Bedouin Tea (Shai):
No visit to Petra is complete without savoring a cup of traditional Bedouin tea, known as "shai." Bedouin tea is made with black tea leaves steeped in boiling water and flavored with fresh mint leaves and sugar, creating a fragrant and

refreshing beverage that is enjoyed throughout the day, especially during social gatherings and hospitality rituals.

6.1.7. Jordanian Desserts:

Indulge your sweet tooth with traditional Jordanian desserts such as knafeh (sweet cheese pastry soaked in syrup), baklava (layers of phyllo pastry filled with nuts and honey), and qatayef (stuffed pancakes filled with sweet cheese or nuts), which are available at local bakeries and sweet shops in Petra.

Exploring the culinary delights of Petra is a delightful journey of flavors, aromas, and cultural discovery. From savory stews and grilled meats to fragrant teas and indulgent desserts, Petra's local dishes offer a tantalizing glimpse into the rich culinary heritage of Jordan. Whether you're dining in a local restaurant, enjoying street food from a market vendor, or sharing a meal with Bedouin hosts, the flavors of Petra will leave a lasting impression on your taste buds and memories of your journey through this ancient and enchanting land.

6.2 Popular Restaurants and Cafes

Petra, with its ancient wonders and breathtaking landscapes, also offers a delightful culinary scene, with restaurants and cafés that cater to a wide range of tastes and preferences. Whether you're craving traditional Jordanian cuisine, international flavors, or a cozy café atmosphere, Petra has something to satisfy every palate. Here's an extensive guide to some of the most popular restaurants and cafés in Petra:

6.2.1. The Cave Bar:

Location: Petra Guest House Hotel, Wadi Musa
Description: The Cave Bar is a unique dining experience located within the Petra Guest House Hotel, offering guests the opportunity to dine in a historical cave setting. The restaurant serves a variety of international and Middle Eastern dishes, including grilled meats, seafood, salads, and vegetarian options. Guests can enjoy their meal surrounded by ancient rock formations and

candlelit ambiance, creating a memorable dining experience in the heart of Petra.

6.2.2. The Basin Restaurant:

Location: Movenpick Resort Petra, Wadi Musa
Description: The Basin Restaurant, located within the Movenpick Resort Petra, offers a luxurious dining experience with panoramic views of Petra's majestic landscape. The restaurant features an extensive menu of international and Jordanian cuisine, with dishes prepared using locally sourced ingredients and traditional recipes. Guests can enjoy a fine dining experience with attentive service and stunning views of the surrounding mountains and valleys.

6.2.3. Al Qantarah Restaurant:

Location: Al Qantarah Hotel, Wadi Musa
Description: Al Qantarah Restaurant is a popular dining spot in Wadi Musa, known for its authentic Jordanian cuisine and warm hospitality. The restaurant offers a variety of traditional dishes, including mansaf, maglouba, and mezze, as well as grilled meats, kebabs, and vegetarian options. Guests can dine indoors in a cozy and welcoming atmosphere or enjoy al fresco dining on the outdoor terrace with views of the city and surrounding mountains.

6.2.4. The Red Cave Restaurant:
Location: Petra Moon Hotel, Wadi Musa

Description: The Red Cave Restaurant, located within the Petra Moon Hotel, offers a unique dining experience in a cave-like setting with warm, rustic décor and traditional Jordanian hospitality. The restaurant serves a variety of local and international dishes, including grilled meats, salads, mezze, and seafood, as well as vegetarian options. Guests can enjoy their meal in a cozy and intimate atmosphere, with attentive service and a selection of local wines and beverages.

6.2.5. Petra Kitchen:

Location: Wadi Musa

Description: Petra Kitchen offers a hands-on culinary experience where guests can learn to cook traditional Jordanian dishes under the guidance of local chefs. The cooking class begins with a visit to the local market to select fresh ingredients, followed by a cooking demonstration and interactive session in the kitchen. Participants learn to prepare dishes such as mansaf, maqluba, and falafel, before enjoying their creations in a communal dining experience with fellow travelers.

6.2.6. Cave Tea House:

Location: Wadi Musa
Description: Cave Tea House is a charming café located in the heart of Wadi Musa, offering a cozy and inviting atmosphere for guests to relax

and unwind after a day of exploring Petra. The café serves a variety of hot and cold beverages, including traditional Bedouin tea, Arabic coffee, herbal teas, and freshly squeezed juices, as well as light snacks and desserts. Guests can enjoy their drinks indoors in a cozy seating area or outdoors on the terrace with views of the city and surrounding mountains.

6.2.7. Nabataean Tent Restaurant:

Location: Wadi Musa

Description: Nabataean Tent Restaurant offers a unique dining experience in a traditional Bedouin tent setting, where guests can enjoy authentic Jordanian cuisine and hospitality. The restaurant serves a variety of grilled meats, rice dishes, salads, and mezze, as well as traditional Bedouin specialties such as zarb and mansaf. Guests can dine under the stars in a magical desert atmosphere, with live music and entertainment adding to the ambiance.

Exploring the culinary scene of Petra is a delightful journey of flavors, aromas, and cultural discovery. Whether you're dining in a cave restaurant, savoring traditional Jordanian dishes, or enjoying a cup of Bedouin tea in a cozy café, Petra offers a diverse and memorable dining experience that reflects the warmth, hospitality, and culinary heritage of Jordanian culture.

6.3 Street Food Experiences

Street food in Petra is not just a culinary adventure; it's a vibrant beauty of flavors, aromas, and cultural heritage that reflects the diversity and richness of Jordanian cuisine. From savory snacks and sweet treats to aromatic spices and refreshing beverages, Petra's street food scene offers a delightful array of culinary delights for visitors to savor and enjoy. Here's an extensive guide to the street food experiences you must indulge in while exploring Petra:

6.3.1. Falafel:
Falafel is a beloved Middle Eastern street food made from ground chickpeas or fava beans, mixed with herbs and spices, formed into balls or patties, and deep-fried until crispy and golden brown. Served in a pita pocket or on a platter with tahini sauce, fresh vegetables, and pickles, falafel is a satisfying and flavorful snack that's perfect for munching on while exploring Petra's ancient ruins and attractions.

6.3.2. Shawarma:
Shawarma is a popular street food in Jordan, consisting of thinly sliced marinated meat (typically chicken, beef, or lamb) roasted on a

vertical rotisserie and served wrapped in a warm pita bread with garlic sauce, pickles, and vegetables. The juicy and flavorful meat, combined with the creamy sauce and crunchy vegetables, makes shawarma a delicious and satisfying meal on the go.

6.3.3. Sfiha:

Sfiha, also known as "Arabic pizza," is a savory pastry topped with minced meat, onions, tomatoes, and spices, then baked to perfection. Sfiha is a popular street food snack in Petra, enjoyed hot and fresh from local bakeries and street vendors, making it a tasty and convenient option for hungry travelers exploring the city's sights and attractions.

6.3.4. Fresh Fruit Juices:

Quench your thirst with refreshing fruit juices made from locally grown produce such as oranges, pomegranates, and strawberries. Street vendors in Petra offer a variety of freshly squeezed juices, served cold and packed with vitamins and flavor, making them the perfect beverage to enjoy on a hot day of sightseeing in Petra.

6.3.5. Knafeh:

Knafeh is a beloved Middle Eastern dessert made from shredded phyllo dough, layered with sweet cheese or cream, soaked in syrup, and baked until golden and crispy. Served warm and topped with crushed pistachios or almonds, knafeh is a decadent and indulgent treat that's sure to satisfy your sweet tooth while exploring the streets of Petra.

6.3.6. Arabic Coffee (Qahwa):

Experience the warmth and hospitality of Jordanian culture with a cup of traditional Arabic coffee, known as "qahwa." Served strong and flavored with cardamom, Arabic coffee is a popular beverage in Petra, enjoyed by locals and visitors alike as a symbol of friendship and hospitality.

6.3.7. Roasted Nuts and Seeds:

Roasted nuts and seeds are a popular street food snack in Petra, offering a crunchy and nutritious option for hungry travelers on the go. Vendors roast a variety of nuts and seeds, such as almonds, pistachios, sunflower seeds, and pumpkin seeds, with spices and seasonings, creating a flavorful and satisfying snack that's perfect for munching on while exploring Petra's attractions.

Exploring the street food scene in Petra is a delicious journey of discovery, where every bite tells a story of tradition, culture, and flavor. Whether you're sampling savory falafel, indulging in sweet knafeh, or sipping on aromatic Arabic coffee, Petra's street food experiences offer a tantalizing glimpse into the culinary heritage of Jordan and provide a memorable and delicious way to immerse yourself in the sights, sounds, and flavors of this ancient and enchanting city.

7.0 Exploring Petra

7.1 Overview Map of Petra

Creating an extensive overview map of Petra requires careful consideration of the site's layout, key landmarks, trails, and access points to help visitors navigate and explore this ancient city effectively. Here's a detailed overview map of Petra:

7.1.1. Main Entrance and Visitor Center:
The map should indicate the location of the main entrance and visitor center, where visitors can purchase tickets, obtain information, and access amenities such as restrooms, shops, and cafes.

7.1.2. Siq (Main Entrance Gorge):

Highlight the Siq, a narrow gorge that serves as the main entrance to Petra. This iconic pathway, flanked by towering cliffs, leads visitors on a dramatic journey into the heart of the ancient city.

7.1.3. Treasury (Al-Khazneh):
Mark the Treasury (Al-Khazneh), one of Petra's most famous and recognizable landmarks. This elaborately carved sandstone facade, carved into the cliffside, is a must-see attraction for visitors exploring Petra.

7.1.4. Street of Facades:
Indicate the Street of Facades, a row of monumental tombs carved into the rock face, located near the Treasury. Visitors can explore

these impressive structures and marvel at the intricate architectural details.

7.1.5. Royal Tombs:

Highlight the Royal Tombs, a series of monumental tombs and burial chambers carved into the cliffs of Petra's eastern ridge. These impressive structures, including the Urn Tomb, the Palace Tomb, and the Corinthian Tomb, offer insights into Petra's royal heritage.

7.1.6. Theater:
Mark the Theater, an ancient Roman-style amphitheater carved into the hillside of Petra. This well-preserved structure once served as a

venue for performances and public gatherings and offers panoramic views of the surrounding landscape.

7.1.7. Colonnaded Street:

Highlight the Colonnaded Street, a grand avenue lined with columns and flanked by ancient ruins, including temples, markets, and administrative buildings. This thoroughfare was once the bustling heart of Petra's commercial and civic life.

7.1.8. Great Temple:
Indicate the Great Temple, one of Petra's largest and most important religious complexes. This monumental temple complex features a series of

grand staircases, colonnades, and courtyards, offering insights into Petra's religious practices and architectural achievements.

7.1.9. Monastery (Ad Deir):

Mark the Monastery (Ad Deir), another iconic monument of Petra located high in the cliffs overlooking the ancient city. This massive rock-cut facade, similar in style to the Treasury but larger in scale, is reached via a challenging hike and offers stunning views of Petra and the surrounding landscape.

An overview map of Petra provides visitors with a comprehensive understanding of the site's layout, key landmarks, trails, and amenities, enabling them to navigate and explore this ancient city with confidence and ease. By highlighting important points of interest and providing essential information, the map enhances visitors' experiences and ensures a memorable and rewarding journey through Petra's remarkable landscapes and archaeological wonders.

7.2 Main Attractions

7.2.1 The Siq

The Siq stands as the awe-inspiring gateway to Petra, Jordan's crown jewel and one of the world's most iconic archaeological sites. This narrow, winding gorge, flanked by towering cliffs that soar up to 200 meters high, serves as the primary entrance to Petra's ancient city, captivating visitors with its dramatic beauty, geological wonders, and rich historical significance. Here's an extensive exploration of the Siq and its significance in the Petra experience:

1. Geological Formation:
The Siq was formed over millions of years by the natural forces of water erosion, as flash floods carved through the soft sandstone rock, gradually widening and deepening the canyon. The towering cliffs that flank the Siq showcase intricate layers of sedimentary rock, revealing a geological history that spans millennia.

2. Entrance to Petra:
As visitors pass through the Siq, they embark on a mesmerizing journey back in time, following the footsteps of ancient traders, pilgrims, and travelers who once traversed this legendary passage. The Siq serves as a symbolic threshold between the modern world and Petra's mystical realm, setting the stage for the awe-inspiring discoveries that lie ahead.

3. Architectural Marvels:

Along the walls of the Siq, visitors encounter remnants of Petra's past in the form of intricate rock-cut sculptures, niches, and reliefs that once adorned the canyon's cliffs. These architectural marvels, including niches for statues and channels for water flow, offer glimpses into the craftsmanship and ingenuity of Petra's ancient inhabitants.

4. The Treasury Revealed:
As visitors reach the climax of their journey through the Siq, they are greeted by one of Petra's most iconic and breathtaking sights: the Treasury (Al-Khazneh). Emerging from the narrow confines of the Siq, the Treasury's elaborately carved façade comes into view, bathed in the soft light of the morning sun or illuminated by the golden hues of twilight, casting a spellbinding aura over the canyon.

5. Play of Light and Shadow:
Throughout the day, the interplay of light and shadow within the Siq creates a mesmerizing spectacle, casting ever-changing patterns and

hues upon the canyon walls. The shifting sunlight highlights the Siq's natural contours and geological features, transforming the canyon into a kaleidoscope of colors and textures that captivate the senses.

6. Soundscapes of Petra:
As visitors journey through the Siq, they are enveloped by a symphony of sounds that echo through the canyon's depths: the rhythmic clip-clop of horse hooves on the ancient stone pavement, the melodious calls of birds perched high above, and the whispers of the wind as it weaves through the canyon's narrows. These auditory cues add to the immersive experience of exploring Petra's mystical landscape.

7. Cultural Significance:
Beyond its geological and architectural wonders, the Siq holds profound cultural and historical significance as the primary access point to Petra, a UNESCO World Heritage Site and one of the New Seven Wonders of the World. For millennia, the Siq has served as a vital

thoroughfare for trade, pilgrimage, and cultural exchange, linking Petra to the ancient civilizations of the Near East and beyond.

8. Conservation Efforts:

In recent years, efforts have been made to preserve and protect the Siq and its surrounding environment, including measures to prevent erosion, manage visitor traffic, and safeguard the canyon's fragile archaeological remains. These conservation initiatives aim to ensure that future generations can continue to marvel at the Siq's beauty and experience the magic of Petra for years to come.

The Siq stands as a testament to the timeless allure and enduring legacy of Petra, inviting visitors on a journey of discovery through one of the world's most extraordinary archaeological wonders. From its towering cliffs and ancient sculptures to its mesmerizing play of light and shadow, the Siq captivates the imagination and transports travelers to a realm where the echoes of history resonate with every step. As the gateway to Petra's mystical world, the Siq beckons adventurers, explorers, and dreamers to embark on a once-in-a-lifetime odyssey through the heart of Jordan's ancient past.

7.2.2 The Treasury (Al-Khazneh)

Standing as a mesmerizing testament to the ingenuity and grandeur of ancient Petra, the Treasury, or Al-Khazneh in Arabic, is the crown jewel of this UNESCO World Heritage Site and one of the most iconic archaeological wonders in the world. Carved into the rose-red sandstone cliffs of southern Jordan, the Treasury's elaborate façade captivates visitors with its intricate craftsmanship, mystical aura, and rich historical significance. Here's an extensive exploration of the Treasury and its enduring allure:

1. Architectural Marvel:
The Treasury is a masterpiece of Nabatean architecture, believed to have been carved into

the sandstone cliffs in the 1st century AD. Its imposing façade, standing at approximately 40 meters tall, features intricate Hellenistic and Eastern architectural elements, including Corinthian capitals, friezes, and decorative motifs that reflect Petra's cosmopolitan influences.

2. The Treasury's Purpose:
While its exact function remains a subject of debate among historians and archaeologists, the Treasury is widely believed to have served as a royal tomb or mausoleum for a Nabatean king or high-ranking official. Its elaborate design and strategic location at the entrance to Petra suggest that it may have also functioned as a ceremonial or administrative building, welcoming travelers and merchants to the ancient city.

3. Elaborate Facade:
The Treasury's façade is adorned with intricate carvings, statues, and reliefs that depict mythological figures, deities, and allegorical scenes from Nabatean and Greco-Roman

mythology. The central niche of the Treasury once housed a towering statue, although its exact identity and significance remain a mystery.

4. Legends and Lore:
The Treasury's enigmatic aura has inspired countless legends, myths, and tales throughout the ages. According to local folklore, the Treasury was once the hiding place of hidden treasures, including the fabled wealth of King Solomon or the riches of an ancient pharaoh. Other stories speak of hidden chambers, secret passages, and lost treasures waiting to be discovered within its ancient walls.

5. The Siq's Grand Finale:
Approaching the Treasury through the Siq, Petra's narrow gorge, is a spellbinding experience that adds to the monument's mystique. As visitors emerge from the confines of the Siq, they are greeted by the breathtaking sight of the Treasury's towering façade, bathed in the soft glow of the morning sun or

illuminated by the warm hues of twilight, creating a magical and unforgettable moment.

6. Conservation Efforts:
In recent years, efforts have been made to preserve and protect the Treasury and its surrounding environment, including measures to prevent erosion, stabilize the rock face, and monitor visitor impact. Conservation initiatives aim to ensure that future generations can continue to marvel at the Treasury's beauty and significance for centuries to come.

7. Cultural Symbolism:
As one of Petra's most recognizable landmarks, the Treasury holds profound cultural and symbolic significance for the people of Jordan and beyond. It serves as a symbol of the country's rich heritage, architectural achievements, and spirit of innovation, inspiring awe and wonder in all who behold its splendor.

The Treasury, with its majestic façade, mysterious allure, and rich historical legacy, stands as a timeless monument to the ingenuity, craftsmanship, and cultural heritage of ancient Petra. As visitors marvel at its grandeur and contemplate its mysteries, they are transported back in time to an era of splendor and intrigue, where the echoes of history resonate through the ages. With its enduring beauty and enigmatic presence, the Treasury continues to captivate the imagination and inspire wonder in all who journey to Petra, a true jewel of the ancient world.

7.2.3 The Street of Facades

Nestled within the rose-red cliffs of Petra, Jordan, the Street of Facades stands as a testament to the grandeur and architectural prowess of the ancient Nabateans. This awe-inspiring thoroughfare, lined with towering rock-cut tombs and facades, offers visitors a captivating glimpse into Petra's funerary traditions, cultural heritage, and rich history. Here's an extensive exploration of the Street of Facades and its significance within the ancient city:

1. Architectural Splendor:
The Street of Facades is a striking avenue adorned with a series of monumental rock-cut tombs and facades that flank its sides. These elaborate structures, carved directly into the sandstone cliffs, showcase the Nabateans' mastery of rock-cut architecture and their ability to create grandiose monuments that blend seamlessly with the natural landscape.

2. Necropolis of Petra:
The Street of Facades serves as the main necropolis, or burial area, of ancient Petra, housing the final resting places of Petra's elite and wealthy citizens. The tombs along the street vary in size, complexity, and decoration,

reflecting the social status and wealth of their occupants.

3. Architectural Styles:
The facades along the Street of Facades exhibit a diverse range of architectural styles and decorative motifs, influenced by Nabatean, Hellenistic, Roman, and Eastern artistic traditions. Visitors can marvel at the intricately carved details, including columns, pediments, friezes, and elaborate doorways, which provide insights into the aesthetic tastes and cultural influences of Petra's inhabitants.

4. Royal Tombs:
Among the most impressive structures along the Street of Facades are the Royal Tombs, a series of monumental burial chambers reserved for Petra's ruling elite and aristocracy. These grandiose tombs, including the Urn Tomb, the Silk Tomb, and the Corinthian Tomb, feature elaborate facades adorned with intricate carvings and architectural embellishments, reflecting the wealth and power of their occupants.

5. Funerary Practices:

The Street of Facades offers valuable insights into the funerary practices and beliefs of the Nabateans. The tombs were constructed to accommodate multiple burial chambers, with some featuring elaborate interiors adorned with frescoes, inscriptions, and funerary offerings that reflected the deceased's status and religious beliefs.

6. Cultural Significance:

As one of Petra's most prominent architectural ensembles, the Street of Facades holds profound cultural and historical significance for Jordan and the wider world. It serves as a tangible reminder of Petra's vibrant past, its cosmopolitan influences, and its role as a thriving center of trade, commerce, and culture in the ancient world.

7. Conservation Efforts:

In recent years, efforts have been made to preserve and protect the Street of Facades and its surrounding environment, including measures to prevent erosion, stabilize the rock-cut structures, and monitor visitor impact. Conservation initiatives aim to ensure that future generations can continue to appreciate and explore this remarkable archaeological treasure.

8. Visitor Experience:
Today, visitors to Petra can walk along the Street of Facades, marveling at the monumental tombs and facades that line its path. Guided tours and interpretive signage provide insights into the history, architecture, and significance of the site, allowing visitors to immerse themselves in Petra's ancient past and uncover the stories of its inhabitants.

The Street of Facades stands as a testament to the architectural achievements, cultural heritage, and funerary traditions of ancient Petra. As visitors wander along this grand avenue, they are transported back in time to an era of splendor and intrigue, where the echoes of history resonate through the towering cliffs and majestic tombs of this ancient necropolis. With its rich history, architectural splendor, and cultural significance, the Street of Facades remains a captivating destination for travelers seeking to uncover the mysteries of Petra's past.

7.2.4 The Royal Tombs

In the ancient city of Petra, nestled amidst the rugged cliffs of southern Jordan, the Royal Tombs stand as a majestic testament to the wealth, power, and architectural prowess of the Nabatean civilization. Carved into the rose-red sandstone cliffs, these grandiose burial chambers served as the final resting places for Petra's elite ruling class, offering insights into the city's royal heritage, cultural traditions, and funerary practices. Here's an extensive exploration of the Royal Tombs and their significance within Petra's archaeological landscape:

1. Iconic Landmarks:

The Royal Tombs are among the most iconic and recognizable landmarks of Petra, drawing visitors from around the world with their grandeur, intricacy, and historical significance. These monumental rock-cut facades, towering high above the surrounding landscape, command attention and admiration, reflecting the wealth and status of Petra's elite inhabitants.

2. Architectural Marvels:
The Royal Tombs exhibit a stunning array of architectural styles, decorative motifs, and intricate carvings that showcase the Nabateans' mastery of rock-cut architecture. Each tomb is uniquely designed and adorned with columns, pediments, friezes, and ornamental details that reflect the cultural influences and artistic tastes of the time.

3. Urn Tomb:
One of the most imposing structures among the Royal Tombs is the Urn Tomb, named for the large stone urn that once stood atop its façade. This grandiose tomb features a towering

entrance flanked by towering columns and intricate reliefs, leading to a spacious burial chamber carved into the rock.

4. Silk Tomb:

Adjacent to the Urn Tomb is the Silk Tomb, named for the richly colored bands of sandstone that adorn its façade, resembling the folds of a silk cloth. This elegant tomb features elaborate carvings and architectural details, including Corinthian capitals and intricate reliefs, that showcase the craftsmanship and artistry of the Nabateans.

5. Corinthian Tomb:

The Corinthian Tomb, another prominent structure among the Royal Tombs, features a façade adorned with Corinthian columns, pediments, and friezes that mimic the architectural style of ancient Greek temples. This imposing tomb, carved into the cliffs with meticulous precision, reflects the Nabateans' admiration for classical art and architecture.

6. Palace Tomb:

The Palace Tomb, situated further along the cliff face, is one of the largest and most elaborate structures among the Royal Tombs. Its façade features a series of towering columns, arched doorways, and intricately carved reliefs that evoke the grandeur of a royal palace, hence its name.

7. Funerary Traditions:

The Royal Tombs offer valuable insights into the funerary traditions and beliefs of the Nabateans, who constructed these elaborate monuments to honor their deceased rulers and elite members of society. The tombs were designed to accommodate multiple burial chambers, with intricate carvings, inscriptions, and funerary offerings that reflected the deceased's status and religious beliefs.

8. Conservation and Preservation:

Efforts have been made in recent years to preserve and protect the Royal Tombs and their surrounding environment, including measures to prevent erosion, stabilize the rock-cut structures, and monitor visitor impact. Conservation initiatives aim to ensure that these architectural marvels remain intact for future generations to appreciate and explore.

The Royal Tombs of Petra stand as enduring symbols of the city's royal heritage, architectural achievements, and cultural legacy. As visitors marvel at these majestic monuments, they are transported back in time to an era of splendor and sophistication, where the Nabateans' ingenuity and creativity are on full display. With their grandeur, intricacy, and historical significance, the Royal Tombs continue to captivate the imagination and inspire wonder in all who journey to Petra, a true treasure of the ancient world.

7.2.5 The Monastery (Ad Deir)

Nestled high in the cliffs of Petra, Jordan, the Monastery, known as "Ad Deir" in Arabic, stands as a towering testament to the architectural prowess, religious significance, and natural beauty of this ancient Nabatean city. Carved into the rose-red sandstone cliffs, this monumental rock-cut facade captivates visitors with its grandeur, mystery, and spiritual aura, offering a mesmerizing journey into Petra's rich history and cultural heritage. Here's an extensive exploration of the Monastery and its significance within the ancient city:

1. Architectural Splendor:
The Monastery is a marvel of Nabatean architecture, believed to have been carved into the cliffs in the 1st century AD. Rising approximately 50 meters tall and 45 meters wide, the Monastery's imposing facade features intricate details, including columns, pediments, friezes, and decorative motifs, that showcase the Nabateans' mastery of rock-cut construction and artistic craftsmanship.

2. Remote Location:

Unlike Petra's other iconic monuments, such as the Treasury and the Royal Tombs, the Monastery is located in a more remote area of the ancient city, requiring a challenging hike along a winding trail that ascends steep cliffs and rocky terrain. This remote location adds to the Monastery's mystique and allure, offering intrepid travelers a sense of adventure and discovery as they make their way to this hidden gem.

3. Religious Significance:

The exact purpose of the Monastery remains a subject of debate among historians and archaeologists, with theories ranging from a temple dedicated to the Nabatean god Dushara to a royal tomb or a monastery for Christian monks. Its remote location and lack of burial chambers suggest a religious or ceremonial function, while its monumental scale and architectural grandeur hint at its importance as a sacred site within Petra's religious landscape.

4. Intricate Details:

The facade of the Monastery is adorned with intricate carvings and decorative elements, including Corinthian columns, floral motifs, and geometric patterns, that reflect a blend of Nabatean, Hellenistic, and Eastern artistic influences. Visitors can marvel at the craftsmanship and artistry of the Nabateans as they explore the Monastery's facade and interior chambers.

5. Panoramic Views:

One of the highlights of visiting the Monastery is the breathtaking panoramic views it offers of Petra's surrounding landscape. From its lofty perch high in the cliffs, visitors can enjoy sweeping vistas of the rugged mountains, deep valleys, and ancient ruins that stretch as far as the eye can see, providing a spectacular backdrop for photos and contemplation.

6. Conservation Efforts:

Efforts have been made in recent years to preserve and protect the Monastery and its surrounding environment, including measures to prevent erosion, stabilize the rock-cut facade, and manage visitor impact. Conservation initiatives aim to ensure that this architectural treasure remains intact for future generations to appreciate and explore.

7. Visitor Experience:
Despite its remote location, the Monastery remains a popular destination for visitors to Petra, who are drawn to its beauty, mystery, and spiritual ambiance. Guided tours and hiking excursions offer visitors the opportunity to experience the Monastery firsthand, immersing themselves in its history, architecture, and natural surroundings.

Conclusion:
The Monastery stands as a symbol of Petra's enduring legacy and cultural significance, offering visitors a glimpse into the ancient city's religious, architectural, and natural wonders. With its majestic facade, remote location, and panoramic views, the Monastery continues to

inspire awe and wonder in all who journey to Petra, a timeless treasure of the ancient world.

7.3 Lesser-Known Sites

While Petra's iconic landmarks such as the Treasury, the Monastery, and the Royal Tombs rightfully steal the spotlight, the ancient city is also home to a wealth of lesser-known sites and hidden gems waiting to be discovered by intrepid travelers. From secluded tombs and ancient dwellings to sacred sites and natural wonders, these hidden treasures offer a glimpse into Petra's rich history, cultural heritage, and natural beauty. Here's an extensive exploration of some of Petra's lesser-known sites:

7.3.1. Garden Temple:

Tucked away amidst the cliffs of Petra's eastern ridge, the Garden Temple is a hidden sanctuary that offers a tranquil retreat from the hustle and bustle of the main tourist attractions. This secluded site features a small temple surrounded by lush vegetation, flowering plants, and ancient olive trees, creating a serene oasis in the heart of Petra.

7.3.2. Lion Triclinium:
Located near the Street of Facades, the Lion Triclinium is a lesser-known dining hall adorned with intricately carved reliefs depicting lions, mythological figures, and scenes of feasting and

celebration. This hidden gem offers a fascinating glimpse into the social customs and culinary traditions of ancient Petra's elite inhabitants.

7.3.3. Renaissance Tomb:
Perched high on a cliff overlooking Petra's central valley, the Renaissance Tomb is a hidden marvel that rewards adventurous travelers with stunning views and architectural splendor. This intricately carved tomb features a unique blend of Nabatean and Greco-Roman architectural styles, reflecting Petra's cosmopolitan influences and artistic heritage.

7.3.4. Snake Monument:
Nestled within the cliffs of Petra's southern valley, the Snake Monument is a lesser-known religious site associated with serpent worship and fertility rituals. Carved into the rock face, this enigmatic monument features serpent motifs, inscriptions, and offerings that provide insights into Petra's ancient religious beliefs and practices.

7.3.5. Al-Habis Fortress:

Located on a hilltop overlooking Petra's main archaeological area, the Al-Habis Fortress is a lesser-known defensive structure that once guarded the city's southern approach. Although largely in ruins today, the fortress offers panoramic views of Petra's surrounding landscape and provides a glimpse into the city's military history and strategic importance.

7.3.6. Wadi Farasa:
Venturing beyond Petra's main tourist trail, visitors can explore the scenic Wadi Farasa, a picturesque valley dotted with ancient tombs, caves, and rock-cut dwellings. This lesser-known area offers opportunities for hiking, birdwatching, and exploring Petra's natural beauty away from the crowds.

7.3.7. Lion Monument:

Carved into the cliffs near the entrance to Petra, the Lion Monument is a hidden gem that pays homage to the legendary Nabatean queen, Al-Khazneh. This intricately carved relief depicts a lioness devouring a prey, symbolizing power, protection, and royalty, and offers a fascinating glimpse into Petra's artistic and symbolic heritage.

7.3.8. Byzantine Church:
Hidden amidst Petra's rocky terrain, the Byzantine Church is a lesser-known religious site dating back to the Byzantine period. This

ancient church features well-preserved mosaics, frescoes, and architectural remains that provide insights into Petra's Christian history and cultural heritage.

Exploring Petra's lesser-known sites offers travelers a unique opportunity to delve deeper into the city's rich history, cultural heritage, and natural beauty. From secluded temples and hidden tombs to ancient fortresses and sacred monuments, these hidden treasures reveal the diverse and captivating stories of Petra's past and present, inviting visitors to embark on a journey of discovery through this extraordinary archaeological wonderland.

7.4 Guided Tours vs. Solo Exploration

Exploring Petra, Jordan, presents travelers with a choice between embarking on a guided tour led by knowledgeable experts or venturing out on a solo exploration of this ancient city's wonders.

Each option offers its own set of advantages and considerations, catering to different preferences, interests, and travel styles. Here's an extensive comparison of guided tours and solo exploration in Petra to help you choose the right experience for your visit:

7.4.1 Guided Tours:

Expert Knowledge: Guided tours are led by experienced guides who are well-versed in Petra's history, archaeology, and cultural significance. They provide valuable insights, historical context, and fascinating anecdotes that enhance the visitor experience and deepen understanding of the site.

Structured Itinerary: Guided tours follow a pre-planned itinerary that covers Petra's main highlights and must-see attractions. This ensures that visitors don't miss out on key landmarks and historical sites, making the most of their time in Petra.

Educational Experience: Guided tours offer a structured and educational experience, ideal for travelers seeking to learn about Petra's history, architecture, and culture in-depth. Guides can answer questions, provide explanations, and offer interpretations that enrich the visitor's understanding and appreciation of the site.

Safety and Security: Guided tours provide a level of safety and security, particularly for first-time visitors or those unfamiliar with the terrain. Guides are knowledgeable about potential hazards, emergency procedures, and best practices for navigating Petra safely.

Group Dynamics: Joining a guided tour allows travelers to meet like-minded individuals and share the experience with a group of fellow explorers. This can enhance the social aspect of the visit and provide opportunities for camaraderie, friendship, and shared memories.

7.4.2 Solo Exploration:

Flexibility and Freedom: Solo exploration offers unparalleled flexibility and freedom to explore Petra at your own pace, following your interests and preferences. Travelers can linger at favorite sites, take detours off the beaten path, and create their own unique itinerary based on personal preferences.

Intimate Experience: Exploring Petra solo allows travelers to enjoy a more intimate and immersive experience, free from the constraints of a group tour. Visitors can savor moments of solitude, contemplation, and connection with the ancient city's history and natural beauty.

Photography Opportunities: Solo exploration provides ample opportunities for photography enthusiasts to capture Petra's stunning landscapes, architectural details, and atmospheric moments without the distractions of a group. Travelers can take their time composing shots and capturing the perfect angles and lighting conditions.

Sense of Adventure: Solo exploration appeals to adventurous travelers seeking to blaze their own trails, discover hidden gems, and uncover off-the-beaten-path treasures within Petra. It offers a sense of adventure, spontaneity, and discovery that can be immensely rewarding for those willing to venture off the tourist track.

Personal Reflection: Solo exploration allows travelers to engage in personal reflection, introspection, and contemplation as they navigate Petra's ancient ruins and natural wonders. It offers moments of solitude and quietude for travelers to connect with themselves and the history of the site on a deeper level.

Whether you opt for a guided tour or solo exploration, visiting Petra promises to be an unforgettable journey filled with discovery, wonder, and cultural immersion. Guided tours offer structured education and expert guidance, while solo exploration provides freedom, flexibility, and intimate experiences. Ultimately, the choice between guided tours and solo exploration depends on individual preferences, interests, and travel styles. Regardless of the option chosen, Petra's timeless beauty and historical significance are sure to leave a lasting impression on all who visit this ancient wonderland.

7.5 Activities in Petra

Petra, with its ancient ruins, majestic landscapes, and rich cultural heritage, offers a wide array of activities for visitors to explore and enjoy. Whether you're a history buff, an adventure seeker, a nature lover, or a cultural enthusiast, there's something for everyone in this extraordinary archaeological wonderland. Here's an extensive guide to the diverse activities you can experience in Petra:

7.5.1. Archaeological Exploration:

Main Attractions: Explore Petra's iconic landmarks, including the Treasury, the Monastery, the Royal Tombs, and the Street of Facades, to marvel at the ancient Nabatean architecture and learn about the city's history and significance.

Off-the-Beaten-Path: Venture off the main tourist trails to discover lesser-known sites, hidden tombs, and ancient dwellings scattered throughout Petra's rugged terrain.

7.5.2. Hiking and Trekking:

Al-Khubtha Trail: Embark on the scenic Al-Khubtha Trail, which offers panoramic views of Petra's main monuments and the surrounding mountains.

Ad-Deir Hike: Challenge yourself with a hike to the Monastery (Ad Deir), a remote and breathtakingly beautiful monument located high in the cliffs of Petra.

Wadi Farasa Trail: Explore the picturesque Wadi Farasa, a lush valley dotted with ancient tombs, caves, and rock-cut dwellings, on a leisurely hiking excursion.

7.5.3. Camel and Horseback Riding:

Camel Tours: Experience the romance of the desert on a camel tour through Petra's ancient pathways, offering a unique perspective on the archaeological site and its surroundings.

Horseback Riding: Take a horseback ride through Petra's main thoroughfares, from the Siq to the Treasury, for a memorable and adventurous journey back in time.

7.5.4. Cultural Immersion:

Bedouin Experience: Immerse yourself in Bedouin culture and hospitality with a visit to a traditional Bedouin camp, where you can enjoy tea, music, storytelling, and authentic Bedouin cuisine.

Petra by Night: Witness the magic of Petra by Night, a unique cultural experience where the ancient city is illuminated by candlelight, creating a mystical atmosphere for an unforgettable evening under the stars.

7.5.5. Photography and Sightseeing:

Photography Tours: Capture the beauty and grandeur of Petra's landscapes, monuments, and architectural details on a guided photography tour led by experienced photographers.

Panoramic Viewpoints: Seek out panoramic viewpoints, such as the High Place of Sacrifice and the Al-Habis Fortress, for breathtaking vistas of Petra's ancient cityscape and surrounding mountains.

7.5.6. Culinary Adventures:

Local Cuisine: Sample traditional Jordanian dishes and delicacies at local restaurants, cafes, and street food stalls in and around Petra, including Mansaf, Maqluba, Falafel, and Bedouin tea.

Cooking Classes: Learn the art of Jordanian cooking with a hands-on cooking class, where you can prepare and savor authentic Jordanian recipes using fresh, locally sourced ingredients.

7.5.7. Wellness and Relaxation:

Spa Retreats: Indulge in pampering spa treatments and relaxation therapies at luxury resorts and wellness centers near Petra, offering a rejuvenating escape from the rigors of travel.

Yoga and Meditation: Practice yoga and meditation amidst Petra's natural beauty and serene landscapes, with guided sessions led by experienced instructors in tranquil outdoor settings.

7.5.8. Shopping and Souvenirs:

Local Markets: Explore the vibrant markets and bazaars of Petra, where you can shop for handmade crafts, jewelry, textiles, spices, and souvenirs crafted by local artisans and Bedouin traders.

Unique Souvenirs: Purchase unique souvenirs and mementos of your visit to Petra, including traditional Jordanian clothing, pottery, ceramics, and handwoven rugs, to commemorate your unforgettable journey.

Whether you're exploring ancient ruins, embarking on outdoor adventures, immersing yourself in local culture, or simply relaxing and enjoying the natural beauty of the surroundings, Petra offers a wealth of activities and experiences to suit every traveler's interests and preferences. With its timeless charm and boundless opportunities for exploration and discovery, Petra promises an unforgettable adventure that will leave a lasting impression for years to come.

8.0 Hiking Trails

8.1 Horseback Riding

Horseback riding in Petra offers visitors a unique and unforgettable way to explore this ancient city's stunning landscapes, archaeological wonders, and rich cultural heritage. Whether you're a seasoned equestrian or a first-time rider, saddling up for a ride through Petra's ancient pathways promises an exhilarating journey back in time. Here's an extensive guide to horseback riding in Petra, including tips, experiences, and what to expect:

8.1.1. Introduction to Horseback Riding in Petra:

Horseback riding has long been a popular mode of transportation for visitors exploring Petra's vast archaeological site. Horses, along with camels and donkeys, provide an alternative means of traversing the ancient city's rugged terrain, offering a unique perspective on its monuments and landscapes.

Experienced local guides and handlers offer horseback riding tours and excursions, providing visitors with well-trained horses, safety equipment, and expert guidance throughout the journey.

8.1.2. Booking a Horseback Riding Tour:

Visitors can book horseback riding tours and excursions through local tour operators, hotels, or directly with guides stationed at Petra's entrance.

It's essential to inquire about the duration of the tour, the itinerary, the condition of the horses, and safety measures before booking to ensure a safe and enjoyable experience.

8.1.3. Horseback Riding Routes and Itineraries:

Horseback riding tours in Petra typically follow established routes that cover the main attractions, including the Siq, the Treasury, the Street of Facades, and the Monastery (Ad Deir). Riders can choose from a variety of itineraries, ranging from short rides to specific landmarks to longer excursions that explore Petra's vast archaeological site more comprehensively.

8.1.4. Riding Experience and Skill Level:

Horseback riding in Petra caters to riders of all experience levels, from beginners to advanced equestrians. Guides and handlers can accommodate riders' preferences and comfort levels, providing gentle horses and tailored instruction as needed.
Visitors with limited riding experience may opt for shorter, slower-paced rides, while experienced riders can enjoy more challenging routes and terrain.

8.1.5. Safety Considerations:

Safety is paramount when horseback riding in Petra. Riders should wear appropriate attire, including closed-toe shoes and helmets if available.

It's essential to follow the guide's instructions, maintain a safe distance from other riders, and respect the horses' behavior and temperament throughout the ride.

8.1.6. Cultural and Historical Commentary:

Horseback riding tours in Petra often include informative commentary from knowledgeable guides, who share insights into the site's history, archaeology, and cultural significance.

Riders can learn about Petra's Nabatean origins, its role as a thriving trade hub, and the significance of its monuments and landmarks as they explore the ancient city on horseback.

8.1.7. Photography Opportunities:

Horseback riding in Petra offers ample opportunities for photography enthusiasts to capture stunning vistas, panoramic views, and close-up shots of the site's architectural details and natural beauty.

Riders can capture memorable moments from unique vantage points while on horseback, creating lasting memories of their equestrian adventure in Petra.

8.1.8. Environmental Impact and Sustainability:

Responsible horseback riding practices, such as staying on designated trails, minimizing disturbance to wildlife, and respecting archaeological sites, help preserve Petra's fragile environment and cultural heritage for future generations to enjoy.

Visitors can support sustainable tourism initiatives and local conservation efforts by choosing reputable tour operators that prioritize environmental stewardship and responsible tourism practices.

Horseback riding in Petra offers a thrilling and immersive way to experience this ancient city's wonders, combining adventure, history, and cultural exploration into one unforgettable journey. Whether you're galloping through the Siq, trotting past the Treasury, or meandering along Petra's ancient pathways, exploring the site on horseback promises an exhilarating adventure that will leave a lasting impression for years to come.

8.2 Camel Rides

Camel rides offer an authentic and unforgettable way to experience the ancient wonders of Petra, Jordan. As one of the oldest and most iconic forms of transportation in the region, camel rides provide visitors with a unique perspective on Petra's majestic landscapes, ancient monuments, and rich cultural heritage. Here's an extensive guide to camel rides in Petra, including experiences, tips, and what to expect:

8.2.1. Introduction to Camel Rides in Petra:

Camel rides have been a traditional mode of transportation in the Middle East for centuries, and Petra is no exception. Riding a camel through Petra's rugged terrain offers a glimpse into the ancient way of life and provides a memorable adventure for visitors of all ages.

8.2.2. Booking a Camel Ride:

Camel rides can be booked through local tour operators, hotels, or directly with camel handlers stationed at Petra's entrance.
Visitors can choose from a variety of camel ride options, including short rides around the entrance area, longer excursions to specific landmarks, or multi-day treks through Petra's desert landscapes.

8.2.3. Camel Riding Routes and Itineraries:

Camel rides in Petra typically follow established routes that cover the main attractions, such as the

Siq, the Treasury, the Street of Facades, and the Monastery (Ad Deir).

Riders can opt for guided tours led by experienced handlers who provide commentary on the site's history, archaeology, and cultural significance along the way.

8.2.4. Riding Experience and Comfort:

Camel rides cater to riders of all experience levels, from beginners to seasoned adventurers. Camels are gentle, docile animals that are well-suited for carrying passengers through Petra's rocky terrain.

Riders should wear comfortable clothing and footwear suitable for outdoor activities and be prepared for the rhythmic swaying motion of the camel's gait.

8.2.5. Safety Considerations:

Safety is a top priority when riding camels in Petra. Riders should listen to the instructions of the camel handlers, maintain a secure grip on the saddle or handlebars, and refrain from making sudden movements that could startle the camels. Helmets may be provided for riders, especially for children or those with safety concerns.

8.2.6. Cultural and Historical Commentary:

Many camel ride experiences in Petra include informative commentary from knowledgeable guides or handlers, who share insights into the site's history, archaeology, and cultural significance.
Riders can learn about Petra's Nabatean origins, its role as a major trade hub, and the significance of its monuments and landmarks as they journey through the ancient city on camelback.

8.2.7. Photography Opportunities:

Camel rides offer excellent opportunities for photography enthusiasts to capture unique perspectives and panoramic views of Petra's archaeological wonders and natural beauty.

Riders can capture memorable moments from the back of their camel, including close-up shots of the Treasury, sweeping vistas of the surrounding landscape, and candid snapshots of their camel companions.

8.2.8. Environmental Impact and Sustainability:

Responsible camel riding practices, such as staying on designated trails, minimizing disturbance to wildlife, and respecting archaeological sites, help preserve Petra's fragile environment and cultural heritage.
Visitors can support sustainable tourism initiatives and local conservation efforts by choosing reputable tour operators that prioritize environmental stewardship and responsible tourism practices.

Camel rides in Petra offer a memorable and immersive way to explore this ancient city's wonders, combining adventure, history, and cultural discovery into one unforgettable experience. Whether you're gliding through the Siq, ambling past the Treasury, or traversing Petra's desert landscapes, exploring the site on camelback promises an exhilarating adventure that will leave a lasting impression for years to come.

8.3 Sunset and Night Tours

As the sun dips below the horizon, casting a golden glow over the ancient city of Petra, a new world of enchantment and mystery emerges under the cover of darkness. Sunset and night tours offer visitors a unique opportunity to experience Petra in a different light, as the illuminated monuments, starlit skies, and tranquil ambiance create a magical atmosphere that's sure to leave a lasting impression. Here's an extensive guide to sunset and night tours in Petra, including experiences, highlights, and what to expect:

8.3.1. Sunset Tours:

Magical Moments: Sunset tours in Petra offer visitors a chance to witness the breathtaking beauty of the ancient city as the sun sets behind the towering cliffs, casting a warm, golden glow over the sandstone monuments and rock-cut facades.

Panoramic Views: Experience panoramic views of Petra's main attractions, including the Treasury, the Monastery, and the Royal Tombs, as the fading light bathes the landscape in a soft, ethereal glow.

Photography Opportunities: Capture stunning sunset photos of Petra's iconic landmarks against the backdrop of the colorful sky, creating unforgettable memories of your visit to this ancient wonder.

8.3.2. Night Tours:

Mystical Atmosphere: Night tours in Petra transport visitors to a world of mystery and intrigue as the ancient city comes alive under the starlit sky. Illuminated by candlelight and moonlight, Petra's monuments take on a magical quality, evoking the spirit of its Nabatean past.

Petra by Night: Experience the enchantment of Petra by Night, a special cultural event where the ancient city is illuminated by thousands of candles, creating a mesmerizing spectacle that's both awe-inspiring and romantic.

Stargazing: Enjoy the opportunity to stargaze in Petra's desert skies, far from the glare of city lights, and marvel at the constellations, planets, and celestial wonders that adorn the heavens above.

8.3.3. Highlights of Sunset and Night Tours:

The Treasury: Watch as the Treasury, Petra's most iconic monument, is bathed in the warm hues of the setting sun, creating a magical backdrop for photos and contemplation.

The Monastery (Ad Deir): Witness the awe-inspiring beauty of the Monastery illuminated against the night sky, its towering facade illuminated by candlelight or moonlight, creating a dramatic and unforgettable sight.

The Siq: Walk through the narrow canyon of the Siq as the fading light casts mysterious shadows on the towering cliffs, creating an atmospheric and immersive experience.

8.3.4. Cultural Experiences:

Bedouin Music and Dance: Enjoy traditional Bedouin music and dance performances under the stars, where local musicians and dancers entertain visitors with lively rhythms and mesmerizing movements.

Storytelling and Folklore: Listen to captivating stories and folklore tales about Petra's history, legends, and mysteries, shared by knowledgeable guides and storytellers who bring the ancient city's past to life.

8.3.5. Practical Considerations:

Clothing and Footwear: Dress warmly and wear comfortable footwear suitable for walking on uneven terrain, as temperatures can drop after sunset and some areas of Petra may be dimly lit.

Safety: Follow the instructions of your guides and stay within designated areas during the tour to ensure your safety and minimize the risk of accidents or injury.

Booking: Sunset and night tours in Petra may require advance booking, especially during peak tourist seasons or special events such as Petra by Night. Be sure to check availability and make reservations in advance to secure your spot.

8.3.6. Environmental Awareness:

Responsible Tourism: Practice responsible tourism by respecting Petra's fragile environment and cultural heritage during your visit. Avoid littering, damaging archaeological sites, or disturbing wildlife, and follow Leave No Trace principles to minimize your impact on the landscape.

Conclusion:

Sunset and night tours in Petra offer a magical and immersive experience that allows visitors to see this ancient city in a new light. From witnessing the beauty of Petra's monuments at sunset to exploring its mysteries under the cover of darkness, these tours provide unforgettable memories and create lasting impressions that will stay with you long after your visit to this extraordinary archaeological wonder.

9.0 Cultural and Historical Insights

9.1 Nabatean Civilization

The Nabateans, an ancient Arab people who flourished from the 4th century BCE to the 1st century CE, left an indelible mark on history with their remarkable civilization centered around the city of Petra in present-day Jordan. Renowned for their mastery of trade, architecture, and water management, the Nabateans were influential players in the ancient world, forging a vibrant and prosperous society that thrived amidst the harsh desert landscapes of the Arabian Peninsula. Here's an extensive exploration of the Nabatean civilization, its history, culture, achievements, and enduring legacy:

9.1.1. Origins and Early History:

The origins of the Nabatean civilization can be traced back to the nomadic tribes of the Arabian

Peninsula, who inhabited the desert regions of present-day Jordan, Saudi Arabia, and Israel.

The Nabateans gradually emerged as a distinct ethnic and cultural group, establishing permanent settlements and trading networks along strategic caravan routes that linked the Arabian Peninsula with the Mediterranean world.

9.1.2. Rise of Petra:

The Nabateans' crowning achievement was the city of Petra, which served as their capital and the heart of their civilization. Carved into the rose-red sandstone cliffs of southern Jordan, Petra flourished as a bustling center of trade, culture, and religion.

The strategic location of Petra, at the crossroads of major trade routes between Arabia, Egypt, Syria, and the Mediterranean, allowed the Nabateans to control lucrative trade in spices, incense, silk, and other luxury goods.

9.1.3. Architectural Marvels:

The Nabateans were renowned for their architectural prowess, as evidenced by the stunning rock-cut facades, elaborate tombs, and intricate water management systems they created in Petra and other Nabatean cities.

Petra's iconic landmarks, including the Treasury (Al-Khazneh), the Monastery (Ad Deir), and the Street of Facades, showcase the Nabateans' mastery of rock-cut architecture, artistic craftsmanship, and engineering ingenuity.

9.1.4. Trade and Commerce:

Trade was the lifeblood of the Nabatean civilization, driving economic prosperity and cultural exchange across the ancient world. The Nabateans controlled key trade routes that traversed the Arabian Desert, facilitating the flow of goods between Arabia, India, Africa, and the Mediterranean.

Petra's role as a major trading hub allowed the Nabateans to amass wealth, establish diplomatic relations with neighboring kingdoms, and exert political influence in the region.

9.1.5. Water Management Systems:

The Nabateans' ability to thrive in the arid desert environment of Petra was made possible by their sophisticated water management systems, which included dams, cisterns, and an extensive network of aqueducts.
Ingenious engineering techniques allowed the Nabateans to capture and store rainwater, channel spring runoff, and create reservoirs that sustained agriculture, industry, and urban life in Petra and its surrounding areas.

9.1.6. Religion and Culture:

The Nabateans worshiped a pantheon of deities, including Dushara, the chief god of Petra, and Al-Uzza and Allat, goddesses associated with fertility and protection.
Petra was home to numerous temples, altars, and religious sanctuaries dedicated to Nabatean gods

and goddesses, where rituals, sacrifices, and religious festivals were conducted to honor and appease the divine.

9.1.7. Decline and Legacy:

The decline of the Nabatean civilization began in the 1st century CE with the annexation of Petra by the Roman Empire and the disruption of trade routes due to political instability and economic changes.

Despite the decline of their political power, the Nabateans' legacy endured through their contributions to art, architecture, and commerce, as well as the enduring mystique of Petra, which continues to captivate visitors from around the world to this day.

The Nabatean civilization stands as a testament to human ingenuity, resilience, and creativity, with Petra serving as its crowning achievement and enduring legacy. Through their mastery of trade, architecture, and water management, the

Nabateans transformed the harsh desert landscapes of the Arabian Peninsula into a vibrant and prosperous civilization that left an indelible mark on history. Today, the awe-inspiring ruins of Petra stand as a reminder of the Nabateans' extraordinary achievements and their enduring legacy as one of the most remarkable civilizations of the ancient world.

9.2 Architectural Marvels

Architecture has long been a reflection of human creativity, innovation, and cultural expression, with civilizations throughout history leaving behind a legacy of breathtaking structures that continue to inspire awe and admiration to this day. From ancient wonders to modern marvels, architectural masterpieces serve as tangible symbols of human achievement, ingenuity, and aspiration. Here's an extensive exploration of some of the world's most iconic architectural marvels, spanning different time periods, styles, and civilizations:

9.2.1. Ancient Wonders:

The Great Pyramid of Giza (Egypt): Built over 4,500 years ago, the Great Pyramid of Giza is the last remaining wonder of the ancient world. Its monumental scale, precise engineering, and enduring mystique continue to fascinate and intrigue visitors from around the globe.

The Parthenon (Greece): Perched atop the Acropolis in Athens, the Parthenon is a symbol of classical Greek architecture and the pinnacle of Doric design. Its graceful columns, intricate friezes, and timeless proportions embody the ideals of ancient Greek civilization.

9.2.2. Medieval Marvels:

Chartres Cathedral (France): A masterpiece of French Gothic architecture, Chartres Cathedral is renowned for its soaring spires, exquisite stained glass windows, and intricate sculptural details. It stands as a testament to the skill and craftsmanship of medieval artisans and craftsmen.

Alhambra Palace (Spain): Nestled in the hills of Granada, Spain, the Alhambra Palace is a stunning example of Moorish architecture and Islamic artistry. Its intricate stucco work, geometric patterns, and lush gardens create a tranquil oasis of beauty and serenity.

9.2.3. Renaissance Gems:

St. Peter's Basilica (Italy): Designed by the likes of Michelangelo, Bramante, and Bernini, St. Peter's Basilica is the largest church in the world and the epitome of Renaissance architecture. Its grand dome, majestic façade, and ornate interior make it a masterpiece of Baroque design.

Versailles Palace (France): Built by King Louis XIV, the Palace of Versailles is a sprawling complex of opulent halls, grand ballrooms, and meticulously landscaped gardens. Its lavish architecture and sumptuous décor reflect the extravagance and grandeur of the French monarchy.

9.2.4. Modern Marvels:

Eiffel Tower (France): An iconic symbol of Paris and the epitome of modern engineering, the Eiffel Tower is a towering masterpiece of iron lattice construction. Its graceful silhouette and panoramic views attract millions of visitors each year, making it one of the most visited monuments in the world.
Sydney Opera House (Australia): Designed by Danish architect Jørn Utzon, the Sydney Opera House is a striking fusion of form and function. Its distinctive sail-like shells and sweeping curves have made it an architectural icon and a UNESCO World Heritage site.

9.2.5. Contemporary Icons:

Burj Khalifa (UAE): Soaring over the skyline of Dubai, the Burj Khalifa is the tallest building in the world and a marvel of modern engineering and design. Its sleek glass façade, futuristic silhouette, and innovative construction techniques have earned it international acclaim.

Sagrada Familia (Spain): Designed by renowned architect Antoni Gaudí, the Sagrada Familia is a one-of-a-kind masterpiece of organic architecture and Catalan Modernism. Its intricate façades, towering spires, and awe-inspiring interiors continue to captivate visitors and architects alike.

Architectural marvels are more than just buildings; they are testaments to human imagination, skill, and ambition. From ancient wonders like the Great Pyramid of Giza to modern marvels like the Burj Khalifa, these structures continue to inspire wonder, admiration, and reverence, serving as enduring symbols of human achievement and creativity throughout the ages.

9.3 Religious Significance

Religion has played a central role in shaping human societies, cultures, and civilizations for millennia, giving rise to sacred sites, rituals, and beliefs that continue to inspire devotion, reflection, and spiritual enlightenment. Across the globe, from ancient temples to modern mosques, churches, synagogues, and temples, religious sites serve as focal points for worship, pilgrimage, and communal gatherings, embodying the profound spiritual and cultural significance of faith. Here's an extensive exploration of the diverse religious significance found within these sacred spaces:

9.3.1. Spiritual Sanctuaries:

Temples and Shrines: Temples and shrines are sacred spaces dedicated to worship and veneration, often housing statues, relics, or symbols of divine significance. From ancient Greek temples to Hindu shrines, these structures serve as focal points for prayer, meditation, and religious rituals.

9.3.2. Pilgrimage Destinations:

Holy Cities: Holy cities, such as Jerusalem, Mecca, Varanasi, and Lourdes, hold deep religious significance for believers and serve as destinations for pilgrimage and spiritual renewal. Pilgrims travel from far and wide to visit these sacred sites, seeking blessings, forgiveness, and divine intervention.

9.3.3. Cultural Heritage:

Architectural Marvels: Religious buildings, such as cathedrals, mosques, synagogues, and temples, are often architectural marvels, showcasing the artistic and engineering achievements of their respective cultures. These structures are not only places of worship but also symbols of cultural identity and heritage.

9.3.4. Community and Fellowship:

Gathering Places: Religious sites serve as gathering places for communities to come together in worship, celebration, and fellowship. They provide a sense of belonging and community for believers, fostering bonds of solidarity, compassion, and support.

9.3.5. Moral and Ethical Guidance:

Sacred Texts: Religious traditions are often grounded in sacred texts, scriptures, or teachings that provide moral and ethical guidance for believers. These texts serve as sources of wisdom, inspiration, and spiritual insight, shaping individual beliefs and collective values.

9.3.6. Healing and Redemption:

Rituals and Sacraments: Religious rituals, ceremonies, and sacraments offer believers opportunities for healing, redemption, and spiritual transformation. Baptism, communion, confession, and pilgrimage are examples of sacred practices that symbolize purification, communion with the divine, and renewal of faith.

9.3.7. Interfaith Dialogue:

Shared Values: Despite differences in beliefs and practices, many religions share common values, such as compassion, justice, and love for humanity. Interfaith dialogue fosters mutual understanding, respect, and cooperation among religious communities, promoting peace, harmony, and reconciliation.

9.3.8. Environmental Stewardship:

Sacred Nature: In many religious traditions, nature is revered as sacred, reflecting divine presence and spiritual interconnectedness. Sacred mountains, rivers, forests, and groves serve as places of worship and contemplation, inspiring reverence for the natural world and a sense of environmental stewardship.

Religious significance transcends boundaries of time, culture, and geography, touching the hearts and souls of believers around the world. From the awe-inspiring architecture of cathedrals to the serene beauty of Buddhist temples, religious sites embody the spiritual aspirations, cultural heritage, and shared humanity of humanity. Through prayer, pilgrimage, ritual, and community, believers find solace, meaning, and purpose in the sacred spaces that illuminate their faith journey and deepen their connection to the divine.

9.4 Petra in Popular Culture

Petra, with its stunning rock-cut architecture, ancient monuments, and dramatic landscapes, has captured the imagination of people around the world for centuries. This UNESCO World Heritage Site, nestled in the desert of southern Jordan, has served as a backdrop for numerous works of literature, film, art, and popular culture, inspiring awe, fascination, and intrigue. Here's an extensive exploration of Petra's presence in popular culture and its enduring legacy as a symbol of wonder and mystery:

9.4.1. Literary References:

"Indiana Jones and the Last Crusade" (Film): Perhaps one of the most iconic depictions of Petra in popular culture is its appearance in the film "Indiana Jones and the Last Crusade." In the movie, Petra's Treasury serves as the entrance to the fictional "Canyon of the Crescent Moon," where Indiana Jones seeks the Holy Grail.
"The Rose-Red City" (Poem by John William Burgon): In the 19th century, English poet John William Burgon penned the famous poem "Petra," in which he describes the ancient city as the "rose-red city" half as old as time, immortalizing its beauty and grandeur in verse.

9.4.2. Film and Television:

"Transformers: Revenge of the Fallen" (Film): Petra makes a cameo appearance in the blockbuster film "Transformers: Revenge of the Fallen," where it serves as the location of one of the climactic battle scenes between the Autobots and Decepticons.
"The Mummy Returns" (Film): While not explicitly mentioned, the fictional city of Hamunaptra in "The Mummy Returns" bears a striking resemblance to Petra, with its ancient ruins and hidden tombs serving as the backdrop for the film's action-packed adventure.

9.4.3. Art and Photography:

Paintings and Drawings: Petra's iconic Treasury, Monastery, and other landmarks have been immortalized in countless paintings, drawings, and sketches by artists inspired by its awe-inspiring beauty and architectural splendor.

Photography: Photographers from around the world flock to Petra to capture its breathtaking vistas, intricate carvings, and dramatic landscapes, preserving its timeless allure through stunning images that grace the pages of magazines, books, and online galleries.

9.4.4. Music and Literature:

Songs and Albums: Petra's mystical aura and ancient allure have inspired musicians and songwriters to incorporate its imagery and symbolism into their music. From rock bands to classical composers, Petra's influence can be heard in songs and albums that evoke a sense of adventure, mystery, and discovery.

Novels and Travel Writing: Writers and authors have penned novels, travelogues, and guidebooks that feature Petra as a central setting or point of inspiration. These literary works capture the essence of Petra's history, culture, and significance, inviting readers to embark on their own journey of exploration and discovery.

9.4.5. Tourism and Popular Imagery:

Postcards and Souvenirs: Petra's iconic Treasury, carved into the rose-red cliffs, is a popular image on postcards, posters, and souvenirs sold in gift shops and tourist markets around the world. These iconic representations serve as mementos of visitors' experiences and memories of Petra.
Travel Documentaries and Television Shows: Documentaries and television programs that showcase Petra's beauty, history, and significance as an archaeological wonder attract viewers eager to learn more about this ancient marvel and its cultural heritage.

9.4.6. Cultural Influence and Symbolism:

Symbol of Adventure and Exploration: Petra has come to symbolize adventure, exploration, and the allure of the unknown, captivating imaginations and inspiring dreams of discovery for generations of travelers, adventurers, and explorers.

Cultural Heritage and Legacy: As a UNESCO World Heritage Site, Petra holds immense cultural significance as a testament to human ingenuity, creativity, and resilience. Its preservation and protection serve as a reminder of the importance of safeguarding our shared heritage for future generations to cherish and enjoy.

Petra's presence in popular culture is a testament to its enduring appeal as a timeless icon of wonder and mystery. From its appearances in films and literature to its influence on art, music, and travel, Petra continues to captivate and inspire people around the world, drawing them into its ancient embrace and inviting them to explore its hidden treasures and timeless beauty. As a symbol of adventure, exploration, and cultural heritage, Petra's legacy will continue to shine brightly for generations to come.

10.0 Practical Tips

10.1 Language and Communication

Language is one of humanity's most powerful tools, serving as a vehicle for communication, expression, and understanding across cultures, continents, and centuries. From spoken words to written texts, sign language to digital communication, language shapes our thoughts, beliefs, and interactions, forming the foundation of human society and civilization. Here's an extensive exploration of language and communication, its evolution, diversity, and profound impact on the human experience:

10.1.1. Evolution of Language:

Origins and Development: The origins of human language are shrouded in mystery, with scholars debating when and how our ancestors first began to communicate through spoken words. Over millennia, languages evolved and diversified, adapting to new environments, cultures, and social contexts.

Language Families: Languages are grouped into families based on shared linguistic features and historical connections. Examples include the Indo-European, Afro-Asiatic, and Sino-Tibetan language families, which encompass thousands of languages spoken by diverse communities around the world.

10.1.2. Diversity of Languages:

Global Linguistic Diversity: There are an estimated 7,000 languages spoken worldwide, each with its own unique grammar, vocabulary, and pronunciation. From major world languages like English, Mandarin Chinese, and Spanish to endangered indigenous languages spoken by small communities, linguistic diversity reflects the richness and complexity of human culture.

Endangered Languages: Many languages are at risk of extinction due to globalization, urbanization, and cultural assimilation. Efforts to document, preserve, and revitalize endangered languages are underway to safeguard linguistic diversity and cultural heritage for future generations.

10.1.3. Functions of Language:

Communication: At its core, language facilitates communication between individuals and groups, allowing them to convey thoughts, emotions, desires, and information through spoken, written, or signed symbols.

Expression: Language serves as a medium for self-expression, creativity, and artistic communication, enabling individuals to share their thoughts, feelings, and experiences through literature, poetry, music, and other forms of cultural expression.

10.1.4. Modes of Communication:

Spoken Language: Spoken language is the most common mode of communication, involving the production and reception of sounds, words, and sentences through the vocal apparatus. It allows for real-time interaction and dialogue between speakers and listeners.

Written Language: Written language involves the representation of spoken words and sounds through symbols, characters, or alphabets. It enables communication across time and space, allowing for the preservation and dissemination of knowledge, ideas, and stories through texts, books, and digital media.

10.1.5. Nonverbal Communication:

Body Language: Nonverbal communication encompasses gestures, facial expressions, posture, and eye contact, which convey meaning and emotions without the use of words. It plays a crucial role in interpersonal communication and can complement or contradict spoken language.

Sign Language: Sign languages are visual-spatial languages used by deaf and hard-of-hearing individuals to communicate through handshapes, movements, and facial expressions. They have their own grammatical rules and syntax and are recognized as fully-fledged languages in their own right.

10.1.6. Technology and Communication:

Digital Communication: Advances in technology have transformed the way we communicate, enabling instant, global communication through email, social media, messaging apps, and video conferencing platforms. Digital communication has made it easier to connect with others across distances and cultural boundaries, but also raises concerns about privacy, security, and digital divide.

Machine Translation: Machine translation tools, such as Google Translate, use artificial intelligence to translate text between languages, facilitating cross-cultural communication and breaking down language barriers in real-time. However, the accuracy and nuance of machine translation still lag behind human proficiency, leading to potential misunderstandings and errors.

10.1.7. Language and Identity:

Cultural Identity: Language is deeply intertwined with cultural identity, shaping how individuals perceive themselves and others within their communities. Bilingualism, multilingualism, and language revitalization efforts play a vital role in preserving cultural heritage and promoting linguistic diversity.
Language Revitalization: Efforts to revitalize endangered languages often involve community-based initiatives, language immersion programs, and educational resources aimed at promoting language pride, proficiency, and intergenerational transmission.

10.1.8. Language and Power:

Linguistic Hegemony: Dominant languages, such as English, French, and Mandarin Chinese, often hold significant economic, political, and cultural power on a global scale, influencing education, media, trade, and diplomacy. This can lead to linguistic imperialism and the marginalization of minority languages and cultures.

Language Policy: Language policies implemented by governments and institutions can shape language use, education, and representation within society, either promoting linguistic diversity and inclusion or reinforcing linguistic hierarchies and inequalities.

10.1.9 Basic petra phrases

When visiting Petra, Jordan, embracing the local language can enhance your experience, foster connections with locals, and show respect for the culture and traditions of the region. While English is widely spoken in tourist areas, learning a few basic phrases in Arabic can go a long way in making your journey more meaningful and enjoyable. Here's an extensive guide to essential Petra phrases to help you navigate your visit with confidence and cultural sensitivity:

1. Greetings and Courtesies:

Hello: مرحباً (Marhaban)
Good morning: صباح الخير (Sabah al-khayr)
Good afternoon: مساء الخير (Masa' al-khayr)
Good evening: مساء الخير (Masa' al-khayr)
Thank you: شكراً (Shukran)
You're welcome: على الرحب والسعة (Ala al-rahb wa al-sa'ah)
Please: من فضلك (Min fadlik)
Excuse me: عذراً (A'zran)

2. Basic Communication:

Yes: نعم (Na'am)
No: لا (La)
I don't understand: أنا لا أفهم (Ana la afham)
Can you help me?: هل يمكنك مساعدتي؟ (Hal yumkinuka musa'adati?)
Where is...?: أين...؟ (Ayna...?)
How much is this?: كم ثمن هذا؟ (Kam thamanu hatha?)
I need...: أحتاج إلى... (Ahtaju ila...)
I'm sorry: آسف (Asif)

3. Directions and Navigation:

Where is Petra?: أين البتراء؟ (Ayna al-Batra?)
How do I get to...?: كيف يمكنني الوصول إلى...؟ (Kayfa yumkinuni al-wusul ila...?)
Left: اليسار (Al-yasar)
Right: اليمين (Al-yameen)
Straight ahead: مباشرة (Mubashirah)
Nearby: قريب (Qareeb)
Far: بعيد (Baeed)

4. Dining and Food:

Menu: القائمة (Al-qaimah)
Water: ماء (Ma')
Food: طعام (Ta'am)
Vegetarian: نباتي (Nabati)
Meat: لحم (Lahm)
Spicy: حار (Har)
Delicious: لذيذ (Lazeez)

5. Numbers:

One: واحد (Wahid)
Two: اثنان (Ithnayn)
Three: ثلاثة (Thalatha)
Four: أربعة (Arba'a)
Five: خمسة (Khamsa)
Ten: عشرة (Ashara)
Twenty: عشرون (Ishroon)

6. Emergencies:

Help!: النجدة! (Al-najdah!)
Emergency: حالة طارئة (Halat taree'a)
Hospital: مستشفى (Mustashfa)
Police: شرطة (Shurta)
Doctor: طبيب (Tabeeb)
Ambulance: سيارة إسعاف (Sayarat is'af)

7. Expressing Appreciation:

Beautiful: جميل (Jameel)
Wonderful: رائع (Ra'ee)
Amazing: مذهل (Mudhhil)
Incredible: لا يصدق (La yusaddiq)
Breathtaking: يأسر الأنفاس (Ya'sur al-anfus)

8. Farewells:

Goodbye: وداعاً (Wada'an)
See you later: أراك لاحقاً (Araka lahiqan)
Until we meet again: حتى نلتقي مرة أخرى (Hatta naltaqi marrah ukhra)

Conclusion:

Learning basic phrases in Arabic not only enhances your travel experience in Petra but also shows respect for the local culture and traditions. Even a few words can go a long way in bridging cultural gaps, fostering connections with locals, and creating memorable experiences during your visit to this ancient and enchanting city. So, embrace the opportunity to engage with the local language, and immerse yourself in the rich beauty of Petra's vibrant culture and community.

Language and communication are essential components of the human experience, serving as bridges that connect individuals, communities, and cultures across time and space. From the spoken word to digital communication, language facilitates understanding, expression, and connection, shaping our perceptions, interactions, and relationships with the world around us. As we navigate the complexities of linguistic diversity and cultural identity, fostering communication and empathy across languages remains essential for building inclusive, harmonious societies that celebrate the richness of human expression and experience.

10.2 Photography Etiquette

Photography is not only an art form but also a means of documenting moments, preserving memories, and sharing experiences with others. However, in today's digital age where cameras are ubiquitous, it's essential to practice photography etiquette to ensure that we respect the privacy, culture, and sensitivities of those around us. Whether capturing candid shots in public spaces or documenting important events, adhering to photography etiquette helps maintain courtesy, respect, and mindfulness. Here's an extensive guide to photography etiquette:

10.2.1. Respect Privacy and Personal Space:

Ask for Permission: Before taking someone's photo, especially in close-up or intimate settings, always ask for their permission. Respect their right to decline and move on if they're uncomfortable.
Be Mindful of Backgrounds: Avoid capturing individuals in compromising or private situations. Pay attention to what's happening in the background and ensure it doesn't detract from the main subject or invade their privacy.

10.2.2. Be Considerate in Public Spaces:

Awareness of Surroundings: When photographing in public places, be mindful of the people around you and their right to privacy.

Avoid obstructing pathways, causing distractions, or intruding on private moments.

Respect Cultural Sensitivities: In culturally or religiously significant locations, adhere to local customs and regulations regarding photography. Some places may prohibit photography altogether, while others may require modest attire or restricted access to certain areas.

10.2.3. Practice Discretion at Events and Gatherings:

Respect Event Organizers: At events, such as weddings, concerts, or ceremonies, follow the guidelines provided by event organizers regarding photography. Avoid disruptive behavior or interfering with official photographers.

Consider Others' Experience: Be aware of your surroundings and how your photography may impact others' enjoyment of the event. Avoid blocking views, using flash in dimly lit areas, or causing distractions during solemn moments.

10.2.4. Be Courteous to Subjects and Models:

Communicate Clearly: If you're photographing models or subjects, communicate your expectations and intentions clearly. Respect their boundaries and preferences regarding posing, wardrobe, and usage of the photos.

Provide Feedback: Offer constructive feedback and encouragement to models or subjects during the shoot. Make them feel comfortable and respected throughout the process.

10.2.5. Practice Responsible Social Media Sharing:

Obtain Consent: Before posting photos of others on social media, obtain their consent, especially if they're recognizable or the photo is of a private nature. Respect their right to privacy and control over their image.

Tagging and Attribution: If sharing photos of others online, provide appropriate tagging or attribution as requested. Be mindful of the context in which the photos are shared and how they may be perceived by others.

10.2.6. Be Mindful of Photography Gear and Equipment:

Respect Property and Facilities: When photographing in public or private spaces, respect property, facilities, and equipment. Avoid damaging or interfering with property while setting up or adjusting your gear.
Minimize Disruptions: Be mindful of the size and noise level of your photography equipment, especially in quiet or sensitive environments. Use discretion and minimize disruptions to others nearby.

10.2.7. Seek Feedback and Learn Continuously:

Accept Feedback Gracefully: Be open to feedback from others regarding your photography etiquette and practices. Use feedback as an opportunity for growth and improvement in your approach to photography.

Educate Yourself: Stay informed about best practices and guidelines for photography etiquette in different contexts and environments. Continuously educate yourself on cultural sensitivities, privacy laws, and ethical considerations related to photography.

10.2.8. Lead by Example:

Set a Positive Example: As a photographer, lead by example and demonstrate respect, consideration, and mindfulness in your photography practices. Encourage others to follow suit and uphold photography etiquette in their own photography endeavors.
Conclusion:
Photography etiquette is not only about capturing great photos but also about respecting the rights, privacy, and dignity of the subjects and environments we photograph. By practicing mindfulness, empathy, and consideration in our photography practices, we can ensure that our passion for photography enhances, rather than detracts from, the experiences of those around

us. Let's strive to be courteous, respectful, and responsible photographers, preserving moments and memories with integrity and empathy.

10.3 General emergency contact in Petra

When exploring the ancient wonders of Petra, it's crucial to be prepared for any unexpected emergencies that may arise. Whether you encounter a medical issue, require assistance with navigation, or need help in a challenging situation, knowing the appropriate emergency contacts can make all the difference in ensuring your safety and well-being. Here's an extensive guide to general emergency contacts in Petra to help you navigate your journey with confidence and peace of mind:

10.3.1. Jordan Emergency Services:

Emergency Number: 911

Description: In case of any life-threatening emergencies, such as accidents, medical emergencies, or criminal incidents, dialing 911 will connect you to the Jordanian emergency services. This number is accessible nationwide and operates 24/7, providing immediate assistance and dispatching appropriate responders to the scene.

10.3.2. Local Police:

Police Emergency Number: 911
Description: If you encounter any criminal activity, theft, harassment, or safety concerns in Petra or its surrounding areas, you can contact the local police by dialing 911. They will respond promptly to your call and take necessary action to address the situation and ensure your safety.

10.3.3. Medical Emergencies:

Emergency Medical Services (EMS): 911

Description: For medical emergencies, including injuries, illnesses, or accidents requiring urgent medical attention, dial 911 to access emergency medical services. Trained paramedics and emergency responders will be dispatched to provide immediate medical assistance and transport you to the nearest medical facility if necessary.

10.3.4. Tourist Police:

Tourist Police: +962 3 215 6170
Description: The Tourist Police in Petra are dedicated to assisting tourists and visitors with any safety concerns, emergencies, or travel-related issues they may encounter during their visit. They can provide guidance, support, and assistance in navigating unfamiliar surroundings and ensuring a safe and enjoyable experience in Petra.

10.3.5. Embassy or Consulate:

Embassy or Consulate Contacts: Check with your country's embassy or consulate in Jordan for their emergency contact information. In case of emergencies involving passport loss, legal issues, or other consular assistance, contact your embassy or consulate for guidance and support.

10.3.6. Petra Visitor Center:

Petra Visitor Center: +962 3 215 7000
Description: The Petra Visitor Center serves as a central hub for tourist information, ticketing, and assistance in Petra. If you encounter any non-emergency issues, such as lost items, transportation inquiries, or general assistance, you can visit or contact the visitor center for guidance and support.

10.3.7. Local Guides or Tour Operators:

Local Guides or Tour Operators: If you're exploring Petra with a local guide or tour operator, they can often provide assistance and support in case of emergencies. Make sure to have their contact information readily available and communicate any concerns or emergencies promptly.

10.3.8. Personal Emergency Contacts:

Family or Friends: Keep your family members' or trusted friends' contact information handy in case of emergencies. They can provide support, guidance, and assistance from afar and coordinate with local authorities or emergency services if needed.

By familiarizing yourself with these general emergency contacts in Petra, you can navigate your journey with confidence, knowing that help is just a phone call away in case of any unforeseen emergencies. Remember to stay vigilant, follow safety guidelines, and prioritize your well-being while exploring the breathtaking wonders of Petra. With proper preparation and awareness, you can enjoy a safe, memorable, and enriching experience in this ancient and enchanting city.

11.0 Sample Itineraries

11.1 One Week Itinerary

A one-week itinerary in Petra offers a perfect balance of exploration, adventure, and relaxation, allowing you to immerse yourself in the rich history, breathtaking landscapes, and vibrant culture of this ancient wonder. From exploring the iconic archaeological sites of Petra to venturing into the rugged beauty of the Jordanian desert, here's an extensive guide to crafting a memorable one-week itinerary in Petra:

Day 1: Arrival in Petra

Morning: Arrive in Petra and check into your accommodation. Take some time to rest and refresh after your journey.

Afternoon: Visit the Petra Visitor Center to obtain tickets and gather information about the archaeological site. Begin your exploration of Petra with a leisurely walk through the Siq, the narrow gorge that leads to the ancient city.

Evening: Enjoy a traditional Jordanian dinner at a local restaurant and immerse yourself in the vibrant atmosphere of Petra by night, where the Treasury is illuminated by candlelight.

Day 2: Exploring the Main Sites of Petra

Morning: Start early to beat the crowds and explore the main highlights of Petra, including the Treasury (Al-Khazneh), the Street of Facades, the Royal Tombs, and the Great Temple.

Afternoon: Continue your exploration of Petra by visiting the Monastery (Ad Deir) and climbing to the High Place of Sacrifice for panoramic views of the ancient city.

Evening: Relax and unwind with dinner at a local restaurant or café, savoring authentic

Jordanian cuisine and reflecting on the day's adventures.

Day 3: Day Trip to Wadi Rum

Morning: Embark on a day trip to Wadi Rum, a stunning desert landscape known for its towering sandstone mountains and vast open spaces. Enjoy a jeep tour or camel ride through the desert, exploring iconic landmarks like Lawrence's Spring and the Seven Pillars of Wisdom.

Afternoon: Have lunch in a traditional Bedouin camp and experience the hospitality of the local Bedouin community. Learn about their culture, traditions, and way of life in the desert.

Evening: Return to Petra in the evening and relax with dinner and a leisurely stroll through the streets of Petra.

Day 4: Cultural Immersion in Petra

Morning: Dive deeper into Petra's rich history and culture with a visit to the Petra Archaeological Museum, where you can learn about the archaeological discoveries and ongoing research in the region.

Afternoon: Participate in a cultural experience, such as a cooking class, pottery workshop, or traditional music performance, to gain insight into Jordanian customs and traditions.

Evening: Enjoy a relaxing evening at your accommodation or explore the local markets and souks, where you can shop for handicrafts, spices, and souvenirs.

Day 5: Petra Off the Beaten Path

Morning: Venture off the beaten path to discover lesser-known sites in Petra, such as the High Place of Petra, the Garden Temple Complex, and the Roman Soldier's Tomb.

Afternoon: Hike to the scenic viewpoints overlooking Petra, such as the Al-Madras Trail or the Al-Habis Mountain Trail, for panoramic vistas of the ancient city and surrounding landscape.

Evening: Treat yourself to a rejuvenating spa treatment or wellness experience at a local spa or wellness center, indulging in traditional massages and therapies.

Day 6: Day Trip to the Dead Sea

Morning: Embark on a day trip to the Dead Sea, the lowest point on Earth, known for its mineral-rich waters and therapeutic mud. Float effortlessly in the buoyant waters and experience the unique sensation of weightlessness.

Afternoon: Relax on the shores of the Dead Sea and enjoy the healing properties of the mud, which is believed to have skincare benefits and therapeutic properties.

Evening: Return to Petra in the evening and dine at a local restaurant, savoring fresh seafood dishes and Mediterranean cuisine.

Day 7: Farewell to Petra

Morning: Take one last stroll through the streets of Petra, savoring the sights and sounds of this ancient wonder. Visit any remaining sites or landmarks on your bucket list before departing.

Afternoon: Check out of your accommodation and bid farewell to Petra, reflecting on the memories and experiences you've gathered during your journey.

Evening: Depart from Petra with a heart full of memories and a newfound appreciation for the rich history, culture, and beauty of this remarkable destination.

A one-week itinerary in Petra offers a comprehensive exploration of this ancient wonder, as well as opportunities to discover the natural beauty, cultural heritage, and warm hospitality of Jordan. From exploring the iconic archaeological sites of Petra to venturing into the desert landscapes of Wadi Rum and the rejuvenating waters of the Dead Sea, each day offers a new adventure and a deeper understanding of this captivating region. Whether you're a history buff, an adventure seeker, or a cultural enthusiast, Petra has something to offer every traveler, leaving you with memories to cherish for a lifetime.

11.2 Weekend Getaway

A weekend getaway provides the perfect opportunity to escape the hustle and bustle of daily life, rejuvenate your spirit, and discover new experiences in a short span of time. Whether you're seeking adventure, relaxation, or cultural exploration, there are countless destinations and activities to suit every traveler's preferences. Here's an extensive guide to planning the ultimate weekend getaway, filled with excitement, relaxation, and memorable moments:

11.2.1 Choosing the Destination:

Proximity: Select a destination that is easily accessible from your location, minimizing travel time and maximizing your time at the destination.
Interests: Consider your interests and preferences, whether it's beach relaxation, mountain hiking, city exploration, or cultural immersion.
Season: Take into account the season and weather conditions to ensure an enjoyable and comfortable getaway experience.

11.2.2 Planning the Itinerary:

Prioritize Activities: Identify the top activities or attractions you want to experience during your weekend getaway and prioritize them in your itinerary.

Flexibility: Leave room for spontaneity and flexibility in your schedule to allow for unexpected discoveries and experiences.

Balance: Strike a balance between active exploration and relaxation, ensuring that you make the most of your time while also allowing for downtime to unwind and recharge.

11.2.3 Packing Essentials:

Clothing: Pack appropriate clothing for the destination and activities planned, including comfortable walking shoes, layers for changing weather conditions, swimwear, and any specialized gear for outdoor activities.

Toiletries: Bring travel-sized toiletries, sunscreen, insect repellent, and any medications or personal care items you may need.

Essentials: Don't forget essentials such as identification, travel documents, phone charger, camera, and any other items necessary for your comfort and convenience.

11.2.4 Accommodation Options:

Hotels: Choose a hotel that suits your preferences and budget, whether it's a luxury resort, boutique hotel, or budget-friendly accommodation.

Vacation Rentals: Consider renting a vacation home, apartment, or cabin for a more private and personalized experience, especially if traveling with a group or family.

Camping: For outdoor enthusiasts, camping can be a budget-friendly and adventurous accommodation option, allowing you to immerse yourself in nature and enjoy the great outdoors.

11.2.5 Transportation:

Car Rental: Renting a car gives you the flexibility to explore the destination at your own pace and venture off the beaten path to discover hidden gems.

Public Transportation: In urban destinations, public transportation such as buses, trains, or subways may be a convenient and cost-effective option for getting around.

Walking or Biking: Depending on the destination, walking or biking may be the best way to explore local neighborhoods, parks, and attractions while staying active and eco-friendly.

11.2.6 Activities and Experiences:

Outdoor Adventures: Depending on the destination, consider outdoor activities such as hiking, biking, kayaking, surfing, or zip-lining for an adrenaline-filled weekend getaway.

Cultural Exploration: Immerse yourself in the local culture by visiting museums, art galleries, historical sites, or attending cultural events, festivals, or performances.

Relaxation and Wellness: Treat yourself to a spa day, yoga retreat, or wellness experience to unwind, rejuvenate, and pamper yourself during your getaway.

Food and Dining: Indulge in local cuisine, culinary tours, or food markets to savor the flavors and specialties of the destination, from street food stalls to Michelin-starred restaurants.

11.2.7 Budget Considerations:

Set a Budget: Determine your budget for accommodations, transportation, activities, dining, and souvenirs, and stick to it to avoid overspending.
Value for Money: Look for deals, discounts, and packages for accommodations, activities, and transportation to maximize value for money without compromising on quality or experiences.
Splurge vs. Save: Prioritize your spending based on your preferences and priorities, whether it's splurging on a luxury hotel or saving money on accommodations to allocate more budget for experiences and activities.

11.2.8 Safety and Wellness:

Health Precautions: Follow health and safety guidelines, including wearing masks, practicing social distancing, and sanitizing hands regularly, especially in public spaces and crowded areas.

Emergency Preparedness: Familiarize yourself with emergency contacts, medical facilities, and local regulations in case of unexpected emergencies or health concerns during your getaway.

Mindfulness and Self-Care: Listen to your body and mind, and take breaks as needed to rest, recharge, and prioritize your well-being throughout your weekend getaway.

A weekend getaway offers the perfect opportunity to escape the routine of daily life, explore new destinations, and create lasting memories with loved ones or solo. By planning thoughtfully, packing essentials, choosing accommodations, selecting activities, and prioritizing safety and wellness, you can ensure a fulfilling, enjoyable, and unforgettable weekend getaway experience. Whether you're seeking adventure, relaxation, or cultural immersion, there's a destination and itinerary waiting to inspire and delight you on your next weekend escape.

11.3 Budget Traveler's Guide

Traveling on a budget doesn't mean sacrificing experiences or missing out on adventure. With careful planning, savvy strategies, and a sense of adventure, budget travelers can explore the world while stretching their dollars further. From finding affordable accommodations to enjoying local cuisine and discovering hidden gems, here's an extensive guide to help you navigate the world of budget travel:

11.3.1. Pre-Trip Planning:

Set a Realistic Budget: Determine how much you can afford to spend on your trip, including transportation, accommodation, meals, activities, and souvenirs. Research the cost of living in your destination to estimate expenses accurately.

Choose Budget-Friendly Destinations: Opt for destinations where your money can go further, such as countries with lower costs of living, favorable exchange rates, or emerging tourist economies. Consider traveling during the shoulder or off-peak seasons to take advantage of lower prices and fewer crowds.

Flexible Travel Dates: Be flexible with your travel dates to take advantage of cheaper airfares, accommodation rates, and travel deals. Use fare comparison websites and flexible date search tools to find the best prices on flights and accommodations.

11.3.2. Transportation:

Budget Airlines: Look for budget airlines and low-cost carriers for affordable airfare options. Be flexible with your departure and arrival airports and travel dates to find the best deals.

Public Transportation: Utilize public transportation, such as buses, trains, subways, or trams, to get around cities and regions. Many destinations offer multi-day or weekly transit passes at discounted rates for tourists.

Ridesharing and Carpooling: Consider ridesharing services or carpooling with other travelers for shared transportation costs, especially for longer distances or remote areas.

11.3.3. Accommodation:

Hostels: Stay in hostels or guesthouses for budget-friendly accommodation options, especially for solo travelers or those on a tight budget. Hostels offer dormitory-style rooms, communal facilities, and opportunities to meet fellow travelers.

Budget Hotels: Look for budget hotels, motels, or guesthouses that offer affordable room rates without sacrificing comfort or convenience.

Book directly through hotel websites or use online booking platforms to find the best deals.

Homestays and Vacation Rentals: Consider staying in homestays, guesthouses, or vacation rentals for a more authentic and immersive experience while saving money on accommodation costs. Websites like Airbnb, Vrbo, and Homestay offer a variety of affordable lodging options worldwide.

11.3.4. Dining and Meals:

Street Food and Local Markets: Explore street food stalls, food markets, and local eateries to sample authentic cuisine at affordable prices. Look for places frequented by locals for delicious and budget-friendly meals.

Self-Catering: Save money on dining expenses by shopping at local grocery stores or supermarkets and preparing your meals in shared kitchen facilities at hostels, guesthouses, or vacation rentals.

Meal Deals and Specials: Take advantage of meal deals, happy hour specials, and discounted dining options offered by restaurants, cafes, and eateries, especially during off-peak hours or slow periods.

11.3.5. Activities and Sightseeing:

Free Attractions: Explore free or low-cost attractions, such as parks, gardens, museums with free admission days, historical sites, and cultural landmarks, to experience the destination's culture and history without spending a fortune.

Walking Tours: Join free or affordable walking tours led by local guides or volunteer organizations to explore the city on foot, learn about its history, architecture, and culture, and interact with fellow travelers.

Outdoor Activities: Take advantage of outdoor activities and recreational opportunities, such as hiking, biking, swimming, or beachcombing, which are often free or have minimal costs associated with them.

11.3.6. Souvenirs and Shopping:

Shop Local: Support local artisans, craftsmen, and businesses by purchasing handmade souvenirs, handicrafts, and unique gifts from markets, boutiques, or artisanal shops. Bargain politely and respectfully for the best prices.

Practical Souvenirs: Choose practical souvenirs such as postcards, magnets, or locally produced food items that are affordable, lightweight, and easy to transport. Avoid buying unnecessary or bulky items that will add to your luggage weight and expenses.

11.3.7. Safety and Security:

Travel Insurance: Invest in travel insurance to protect yourself against unforeseen emergencies, accidents, or trip cancellations that could disrupt your travel plans and incur additional expenses.

Personal Safety: Stay vigilant and aware of your surroundings, especially in crowded or touristy areas, to avoid pickpockets, scams, or petty theft. Keep your valuables secure and use common sense when navigating unfamiliar destinations.

Emergency Funds: Carry emergency cash or a backup credit card for unexpected expenses or emergencies, such as medical bills, transportation disruptions, or unforeseen circumstances that may arise during your travels.

11.3.8. Cultural Immersion:

Interact with Locals: Engage with locals, learn about their customs, traditions, and way of life, and immerse yourself in the local culture to gain a deeper understanding and appreciation of the destination.

Learn Basic Phrases: Learn a few basic phrases in the local language to communicate with locals and show respect for their culture and customs. Use gestures, smiles, and simple phrases to connect with people and make meaningful interactions.

Volunteer Opportunities: Consider volunteering or participating in community-based projects, cultural exchanges, or sustainable tourism initiatives to give back to the local community and make a positive impact during your travels.

Traveling on a budget is not only about saving money but also about maximizing experiences, connecting with cultures, and creating meaningful memories without breaking the bank. By following the tips and strategies outlined in this budget traveler's guide, you can explore the world affordably while enjoying enriching experiences, authentic interactions, and unforgettable adventures. Remember to plan ahead, prioritize your spending, and embrace the spirit of adventure and discovery as you embark on your budget-friendly travels. With a bit of creativity, resourcefulness, and an open mind, you'll discover that budget travel offers endless opportunities for exploration, discovery, and personal growth, allowing you to create lasting memories and stories to cherish for a lifetime. So pack your bags, set out on your next adventure, and embrace the joys of budget travel as you journey to new destinations and make the most of every moment along the way.

12.0 Conclusion

In conclusion, Petra stands as a timeless marvel, beckoning travelers from across the globe to witness its breathtaking beauty and unravel the mysteries of its ancient past. From the majestic Treasury to the rugged landscapes that cradle its wonders, every step in Petra is a journey through history, culture, and awe-inspiring architecture.

As you venture through the narrow Siq, marvel at the intricately carved facades, and stand in awe of the Monastery's grandeur, may you feel a deep connection to the ancient civilizations that once thrived in this desert oasis. Let Petra's timeless charm and undeniable allure leave an indelible mark on your soul, inspiring you to explore, discover, and cherish the wonders of our world.

Whether you're a history enthusiast, an adventurous explorer, or a seeker of hidden treasures, Petra offers an unforgettable experience that transcends time and space. As you bid farewell to this ancient city, may your memories be filled with the echoes of its past and the promise of future adventures yet to come.

Printed in Great Britain
by Amazon